THE G8'S ROLE IN THE NEW MILLENNIUM

To our good friend, the late Michael Hodges

The G8 and Global Governance Series

The G8 and Global Governance Series explores the issues, the institutions and the strategies of participants in the G8 network of global governance, as they address the challenges of shaping global order in the new millennium. Intensifying globalization is moving many once domestic issues into the international arena, requiring constant international co-operation, and demanding new collective leadership to direct the galaxy of multilateral institutions created in 1945. In response, the Group of Eight, composed of the world's major market democracies, including Russia and the European Union, is emerging as the effective source of global governance in the new era. This series focuses on the new issues at the centre of global governance, from finance, investment, and trade, through transnational threats to human security, to traditional political and security challenges. It examines the often invisible network of G8 and G7 institutions as they operate within and outside established international organizations to generate desired outcomes. It analyzes how individual G7 members and other international actors, including multinational firms and those from civil society, devise and implement strategies to secure their preferred global order.

Also in the series

The G7/G8 System
Evolution, role and documentation
Peter I. Hajnal
ISBN 1 84014 776 8

The G8's Role in the New Millennium

Edited by
MICHAEL R. HODGES
London School of Economics and Political Science

JOHN J. KIRTON
University of Toronto

JOSEPH P. DANIELS
Marquette University

Ashgate

Aldershot • Brookfield USA • Singapore • Sydney

© Michael R. Hodges, John J. Kirton and Joseph P. Daniels 1999

Published by
Ashgate Publishing Ltd
Gower House
Croft Road
Aldershot
Hants GU11 3HR
England

Ashgate Publishing Company
Old Post Road
Brookfield
Vermont 05036
USA

British Library Cataloguing in Publication Data
MK The G8's role in the new millennium
1. Group of Eight (Organization) 2. International economic
relations - Congresses
I. Hodges, Michael R. II. Kirton, John J. III. Daniels, Joseph
P.
337.1

Library of Congress Cataloging-in-Publication Data
The G8's role in the new millennium / edited by Michael R. Hodges,
John J. Kirton, Joseph P. Daniels.
p. cm.
Includes bibliographical references and index.
ISBN 1-84014-774-1 (hardback)
1. International economic relations--Congresses. 2. Economic
policy--Congresses. I. Hodges, Michael R., 1945-1998. II. Kirton,
John J. III. Daniels, Joseph P.
HF1359.G26 1999
337--dc21   99-12584
                                                       CIP

ISBN 1 84014 774 1
Printed and bound in Great Britain by MPG Books Ltd, Bodmin, Cornwall

Contents

PART II: THE FINANCIAL CHALLENGES **93**

PART III: THE BROADER CHALLENGES **141**

List of Tables

List of Figures

List of Contributors

Sir Nicholas Bayne, KCMG is a Visiting Fellow at the International Relations Department of the LSE. As a British diplomat, he was High Commissioner to Canada, 1992-1996, Economic Director at the FCO, 1988-1992, and Ambassador to the OECD, 1985-1988. He is co-author, with Robert Putnam, of *Hanging Together: Cooperation and Conflict in the Seven Power Summits*.

Bronwyn Curtis is Chief Economist of Nomura International in London. She is a well-known commentator on financial market issues and author of numerous articles on economic topics. Previously Global Head of Foreign Exchange and Fixed Income Strategy at Deutsche Morgan Grenfell. She joined Deutsche Bank in London in 1988 after an extensive career in international commodity markets.

Professor Joseph P. Daniels is Associate Professor of International Economics at Marquette University, Milwaukee, Wisconsin, and was Visiting Professor of Economics and International Relations, University of Toronto in 1997-98. An established scholar on the G7 Summit process, he has published widely on international economic policy processes.

Professor Charles Goodhart, CBE is Norman Sosnow Professor of Banking and Finance at the LSE, and a member of the Bank of England's Monetary Policy Committee. He was a monetary adviser at the Bank of England from 1968-1985 and Chief Advisor from 1980. He taught at Cambridge and the LSE and has written extensively on monetary policy, history and institutions.

Dr. Michael R. Hodges was Director of the Centre for Research on the USA and Senior Lecturer in International Relations at the LSE. Formerly Professor of International Relations at Lehigh University, Bethlehem, Pennsylvania, he is the author of books on government/business relations, as well as "More Efficiency, Less Dignity: British Perspectives on the G7".

Professor John J. Kirton is Director of the G8 Research Group, Associate Professor of Political Science and Research Associate of the Centre for International Studies at the University of Toronto. He has advised the Canadian Government on G7 participation and international trade and sustainable development, and is the author and editor of many books and articles on international issues, especially on G7 summitry.

Dr. Ella Kokotsis is a Post-Doctoral Research Fellow at the Centre for International Studies, University of Toronto and Research Coordinator of the G8 Research Group. An expert on G8 Summit compliance, she served as a consultant to the Canadian Government's National Round Table on the Environment and the Economy in the lead-up to the 1995 G7 Summit.

Professor Richard Layard is Director of the LSE's Centre for Economic Performance. An expert on the problems of unemployment and inflation, he has advocated a "Welfare to Work" approach in a series of books and articles. Founder in 1985 of the Employment Policy Institute and Chairman, 1987-1992, he is an expert on skills and inequality and heads an advisory group for the Russian Government.

Professor Alan Rugman is Thames Water Fellow in Strategic Management at Templeton College, Oxford. Professor of International Business at the Universities of Toronto, 1987-1998, Dalhousie, 1979-1987, and Winnipeg, 1970-1978, he is author of numerous books and articles on multinational enterprises and trade and investment policy. He has been an adviser to the Canadian Government and a consultant to major companies.

George Staple, QC was Director of the United Kingdom's Serious Fraud Office from 1992 to 1997. A Partner at Clifford Chance from 1967 to 1992, he rejoined the partnership in 1997. He was Chairman of the Authorization and Disciplinary Tribunals of the Securities Association and the Securities and Futures Authority, 1987-1992 and a member of the Council of the Law Society and its Treasurer, 1989-1992.

Ambassador Koji Watanabe is Executive Advisor to the Japan Federation of Economic Organizations (Keidanren); Senior Fellow at the Japan Center for International Exchange; and Chairman of the Board of Governors of the Asia-Europe Foundation. As a Japanese diplomat, Ambassador to Russia, 1993-1996; to Italy, 1992-1993; Deputy Minister of Foreign Affairs, 1989-1992; and "Sherpa" for the 1990 and 1991 summits.

Preface

MiM

John J. Kirton
Joseph P. Daniels

This book is the product, most immediately of two conferences held in London, England on May 12th and 13th, 1998 immediately prior to the Group of Eight (G8) Birmingham Summit. The first conference, a scholarly symposium on "Explaining G8 Effectiveness", assembled six leading scholars of the G8 and its major issues to give papers, for discussion among themselves, their colleagues and students, of how and why the G8 succeeds as an effective international institution in dealing with the major issues of the day.

The second, a public policy conference entitled, "Jobs, Crime, Money: Challenges for the G8 in 1998", gathered 16 distinguished practitioners and scholars from Europe, North America and Asia. Its purpose was to assess the way in which the G8 could and should best address the global priorities of 1998.

This volume contains the extensively revised papers presented at the scholarly symposium, supplemented by selective contributions from the public policy conference. Yet within its chapters also lie the results of decades of reflection and analysis on G7/G8 and the global challenges it currently confronts, from those who have carefully examined these matters from the inside and from without.

To explore these challenges and the effectiveness of the G8 in dealing with them, this collection combines the talents of leading scholars and analysts of the G7/G8 from several disciplines and regions. Its contributors come from the disciplines of economics, management studies, the international political economy subfield of political science, law and from public service. Their combination in this volume provides a rich and unique synthesis of the contributions of the insights of academic scholars from several disciplines as enriched by those of distinguished policy practitioners of analytic repute.

The contributors to this volume are all senior figures from the three global regions represented in the G8: Europe, North America and Japan. Many have worked in two or more of the three G8 regions or have scholarly interests spanning them all. All authors come from leading universities in their countries, or major public or private sector institutions or are leading experts in their area.

No effort has been made to impose a single interpretive framework, common point of view or artificial concluding consensus on the individual contributions. Rather the introduction outlines in full diversity and richness the wide ranging debate about the G8, the major forces at work in the world as the new millennium approaches, and the new issues and challenges this presents for the G8. The inclusion among the editors and authors of those with widely varying views on the G8 and from differing disciplinary perspectives ensures that this work will present a poignant and productive debate rather than a strained consensus.

Producing such a volume and the conferences that lay behind it required the exceptional contribution of many individuals. We owe much to Sir Nicholas Bayne, the master interpreter of the G7/G8, and one who served as a constant source of intellectual inspiration, practical support and sound judgement in moving this enterprise from an academic planning concept into an accomplished reality.

We are further grateful to other members of the G8 Research Group's Professional Advisory Council, who helped us with recruiting speakers, serving as speakers and providing insightful advice along the way. These include Robert C. Fauver, David Hale, Michael R. Hodges, Alan Rugman and Koji Watanabe.

We owe a particular debt to Robin Griffiths and his colleagues at Clifford Chance, who served as sponsors of the May 13th conference from which some of our material is drawn, provided facilities at their London office for our May 12th Scholarly Symposium, sponsored a dinner for our overseas speakers, and then prepared transcripts of the conference presentations that served as an essential tool in composing some of the chapters in this book. Robin's generosity, unflagging willingness to help and endless good cheer were a critical ingredient in making the conference and this volume possible.

We are also grateful to the superb conference team at Clifford Chance - led by Amanda Jenkins, Corinne Pearson-Evans, and Matthew Brown. They handled the often difficult logistics with exceptional efficiency. Jim Sigman, Colton Alton, and Tim Judy at Real Education in Denver, Colorado deserve thanks for their strong support in helping us enhance the educational experience of the summit. They designed and built an Internet-based seminar program to broadcast the conferences and other events to some 2000 students around the world.

Special praise must go to Steve Muddiman, Jolanta Pilecka, Ross Jardine and their staff at Hewlett Packard in the U.K. Their enthusiasm for our project and Hewlett Packard's leading-edge technical support provided an invaluable backbone to our Internet program.

We further wish to express our gratitude to Maurice Fraser, who gave permission for us to use material from Richard Layard's contribution on, "Employability", in M. Fraser (ed.), *The G8 & the World Economy*, (London: Strategems Publishing Limited, 1998).

We also acknowledge with deep gratitude the enormous contribution of Paul Jacobelli, Co-ordinator of the G8 Research Group. It was his vision, entrepreneurship and perseverance that made our London symposium and conference possible, ensured their successful execution and helped to prepare this volume for publication. We also thank Jane Kim for the long hours of painstaking work required to format the text and charts in this book.

Among the many members of the G8 Research Group who contributed to making this volume and the supporting conferences a success, we wish to highlight the leadership and support of Peter Hajnal, Kunihiro Ito, Sian Meikle, Ella Kokotsis, Carla Angelone, Nancy Scott, Ivan Savic, Cindy Blazevic, Michael Youash, Gina Stephens, Sandra Larmour and Marc Lalonde.

Also of major importance in this effort was the support of colleagues from our partner institutions, notably Jonathan Aronson and Steve Lamy of the University of Southern California's School of International Affairs. We also thank our colleagues at Trinity College, the International Relations Program and the Centre for International Studies: Thomas Delworth, Robert Bothwell, Louis Pauly, Geoffrey Seaborn, Marilyn Laville and Mary Lynne Bratti. Finally, we are grateful to our editor at Ashgate, Kirstin Howgate, whose vision, good cheer and dedication sustained us through the process of converting raw text into a finished book.

On June 17, 1998, three weeks after our conference, Michael Hodges suddenly passed away at the age of 53. We are proud and grateful to have worked with him over the years in the G8 Research Group and on this conference and volume, which were very much his inspiration. His chapter in this volume is not the one he would have written, had he had the time to develop his initial thoughts before his untimely death. But it displays the freshness, insight and critical spirit that characterized his scholarship during a long and distinguished career. To honour his very real contribution and his memory, we have retained his name, as planned, as the lead co-editor of this volume. We dedicate it to him and to all that he stood for as a colleague and friend.

John J. Kirton, Joseph P. Daniels, October 1998

List of Abbreviations

APEC	Asia Pacific Economic Cooperation
ASEM	Asia-Europe Meeting
BCCI	Bank of Credit and Commerce International
BIS	Bank for International Settlements
CEC	Commission for Environmental Cooperation (Montreal)
CLC	Canadian Labour Congress
COC	Council of Canadians
DFAIT	Department of Foreign Affairs and International Trade (Canada)
ECB	European Central Bank
EMU	European Monetary Union
EU	European Union
FATF	Financial Action Task Force
FDI	Foreign Direct Investment
FSRA	Fiscal Structural Reform Act (Japan)
FTA	Free Trade Agreement (Canada and U.S.)
FTAA	Free Trade Agreement of the Americas
FY	Fiscal Year
G3	Group of Three (Finance Ministers/Central Bank Governors - Japan, U.S., Germany)
G5	Group of Five (Finance Ministers)
G7	Group of Seven (Major Industrial Countries)
G8	Group of Eight (G7 with Russia)
G15	Group of Fifteen (Developing Countries)
G24	Group of Twenty-Four (Developing Countries within the IMF)
GATT	General Agreement on Tariffs and Trade
GDP	Gross Domestic Product
GIS	Global Information Society
GNP	Gross National Product
HIPC	Heavily Indebted Poorest Countries
IBRD	International Bank of Reconstruction and Development (World Bank)
IMF	International Monetary Fund

IPE	International Political Economy
LDP	Liberal Democratic Party (Japan)
MAI	Multilateral Agreement on Investment
MPC	Monetary Policy Committee of the Bank of England
NAFTA	North America Free Trade Agreement
NATO	North Atlantic Treaty Organization
NGO	Non-governmental organization
OAS	Organization of American States
ODA	Official Development Assistance
OECD	Organization for Economic Cooperation and Development
OPEC	Organization of Petroleum Exporting Countries
OSCE	Organization for Security and Cooperation in Europe
Qaud	Quadrilateral Trade Ministers Forum (Japan, Canada, U.S. and EU)
SFO	Serious Fraud Office
SIG	Support Implementation Group
SME	Small and Medium-Sized Enterprises
TNC	Transnational Corporations
U.N.	United Nations
U.S.	United States
U.S.S.R.	Union of the Soviet Socialists Republics
UK	United Kingdom
UNCED	United Nations Conference on Environment and Development
WHO	World Health Organization
WTO	World Trade Organization

Introduction

1 The Role of the G8 in the New Millennium

JOHN J. KIRTON AND JOSEPH P. DANIELS

for

Introduction

During the 1990s, the Group of Seven (G7) and now Group of Eight (G8), has attracted a rising crescendo of scholarly and policy criticism as it and the world have confronted a host of new issues and major transformations. The criticisms have centered on the apparent failure of the G7/8 to manage its core economic and financial agenda, to assist Russia in its democratic market transition and integration into the global economy, and to address the new transnational issues and pressures toward regionalism in the world. To many, these charges have acquired added force as the Asian financial crisis moves beyond its regional origins to create economic damage and instability everywhere. Further erosion in the credibility of the summit process will no doubt occur as Russia sits precariously on the verge of financial and even political collapse, as Europe reinforces its regional identity and strategy with the advent of the Euro, and as North America considers building on regional solutions through the North American Free Trade Agreement (NAFTA) in response (Bergsten, 1998; Malmgren, 1998; Hale, 1998).

Amidst such prevailing pessimism and uncertainty, this collection offers a more firmly grounded and optimistic assessment of the outlook for global governance as the transformed world of the new millennium rapidly approaches. It looks beyond the current criticism to examine the underlying transformations now underway in the G8 as an institution and in the world that its seeks to govern. It provides a critical, scholarly assessment of the G8's performance and prospects in addressing the issues that have moved from the domestic stage to the centre of the international agenda as the post cold war world of globalization and deepening integration gives way to the fully global system of the new millennium.

The collection explores the logic of the contemporary critics to offer improved explanations of the circumstances under which the G7/G8

3

is effective in addressing both its traditional subjects and the defining issues
of the emerging era - the sound management of the global financial system
in both its governmental and private sector dimensions, employment and
employability, foreign direct investment and its link with social values, and
transnational financial crime and drugs. In all cases, its analysis is policy
oriented and forward looking, both in anticipating the emerging G8 agenda
in these areas, and pointing to what action the G8 will, can or should take to
contribute to global governance in these realms.

The Approach

To meet these objectives this collection builds on, refines and reaches
beyond the major existing competing theories of G7/8 performance outlined
in Table 1.1 - the seminal "American leadership" model of Putnam and
Bayne, the "concert governance" model of Kirton and Wallace, the "false
new consensus" model of Bergsten and Henning, and the recent "democratic institutional" model of Ikenberry and Kokotsis (Putnam and Bayne, 1987;
Kirton, 1989; Kirton, 1993; Wallace, 1984; Bergsten and Henning, 1996;
Ikenberry, 1993; Kokotsis and Kirton, 1997; Kokotsis, 1998).

The objective is to generate new data and insights that will contribute to the development of general theories of international cooperation in
political economy, enrich institutional analysis in economics, and provide a
foundation to assess and advance proposals for G7/G8 reform as it addresses the issues likely to dominate in the new millennium.

To assess the contemporary relevance of such explanations, this collection goes well beyond the particular issues that have historically high-
lighted the G7 agenda. Rather, it explores the enduring central functions of
the G7/8 as an institution of global governance (notably in co-operation,
compliance and crisis management) in the context of the issues and processes that, now and in the future, will dominate a radically transforming world.
Here it draws on and extends the leading theories of G7/8 and international
co-operation to identify the factors and their interrelationships that are relevant to the G7/8's performance in the new era of proliferating globalization.

To conduct such a far reaching, fundamental and forward-looking
analysis, this work employs a multidisciplinary and multidimensional
approach. It mobilizes the perspectives of political science, economics,
management studies and law. It presents analyses from leading experts of
the G7 and its core issues who are based in Europe, North America and

Table 1.1 Models of G7/8 Cooperation and Compliance

Model A: American Leadership (Putnam and Bayne, 1984, 1987)

1. U.S. assertion of "strong leadership in alignment ... with at least one other major power", (subjective hegemony) as necessary but not sufficient condition;
2. "Reigning ideas and the salient historical lessons as interpreted by leaders in each era" (policy ideas and spasmodic learning favouring a recognition of shared interests, in response to dramatic evidence of policy failure);
3. The absence of electoral uncertainties and presence of domestic cleavages and alignments in key countries allowing "a mutually supportive transnational alliance" (domestic politics).

Model B: Concert Governance (Wallace, 1984; Kirton, 1989)

1. Predominant Capabilities - collectively dominant and internally equal capabilities;
2. Constricted Participation among only and all major powers;
3. Common Principles of major power responsibility, market democracy, and rule of law;
4. Political Control by popularly elected leaders;
5. Crisis Pooling - interdependence and intervulnerability activated by crisis, especially a "second shock".

Model C: False New Consensus (Bergsten and Henning, 1996)

Decline during the 1990s due to:

1. False New Consensus - "a growing consensus within the group that changes in global economic conditions make it impossible for them to pursue" previously feasible initiatives;
2. American decline - "the decline in America's economic and security clout, which partly stems from the end of the Cold War and with America's inconsistent policies and inept performance";
3. Traditional differences among the members, particularly the U.S. and Germany, on several key issues.

Model D: Democratic Institutionalism (Ikenberry, 1993; Kokotsis, 1998)

1. Linked Domestic and International Institutions - powerful domestic departments with defined G7 responsibilities and powerful international institutions which G7 members control;
2. G7 Institutionalization - established G7/8 ministerial and official forums and an institutionalized summit preparatory and follow-up process;
3. Multilateral Regime Nests;
4. Leader Commitment - direct involvement by leaders who give priority to the multilateral co-operation, G7 institutions and its particular issues;
5. Popular Support - high domestic approval for leaders and supportive public opinion for the G7/G8 issue.

Japan and who in many cases have had extensive experience in several regions. It provides the views of scholars whose rigorous academic analyses are infused by the insights gained from present and past involvement in often senior reaches of the policy world. It avoids imposing any single model or methodological perspective to allow each contributor to explore with full freedom how a rapidly changing G7/8 system is addressing the demands that dominate the new world of the coming millennium.

The New World and its Challenges

The rapidly approaching new millennium marks not only a convenient chronological divide to assess the pace of the changes to the world economy and political system brought about at the outset of the 1990s by the end of the cold war, and the resulting processes of globalization throughout newly opened democratic polities and market economies. Rather it is also the opening of a new era of major transformation in the capabilities and foreign policy approaches of the world's major powers, the processes which underlie these changes, the agenda created by them, and the way international institutions such as the G7/8 adapt to exercise global governance in response.

The signs of this emergent new system are first evident in the unprecedented and often puzzling changes that arise when the contemporary world is viewed through the traditional state-centric prism of international politics and the management of the international economy. The United States appears, for the first time since the late 1940s, to be enjoying a new across-the board hegemonic dominance, one more deep and enduring than the shallow, short-lived Reagan revival of the early 1980s, but one without the outward looking internationalism of America's initial hegemonic moment (Mulford, 1998). This new America represents a profound challenge to a G7/8 initially created in 1975 in response to American weakness, as a forum where the domestic policy approaches of all members could be shared as valid models, and the domestic resources of all pooled to provide the global public goods America could no longer afford to give alone.

A once vibrant and steadily growing Japan has now endured close to a decade of stagnation and is entering a recession and crisis of confidence that threatens to go well beyond the temporary and limited reversal of the 1973 Organization of Petroleum Exporting Countries (OPEC) oil shock that beset it immediately prior to its entry, as a founding member, into the G7.

Germany, France and Italy, with the advent of the Euro, are moving into an unprecedentedly deep stage and form of regional integration, while Britain and Canada confront the cruel choice of whether to embrace such regionalism or continue as countries with an autonomous global approach in which the institutions of the G7/8 occupy pride of place. And Russia, admitted as a full member to the new G8 that was created alongside the continuing G7 at Birmingham in May 1998, is no longer the threatening cold war power of old nor the stable market democracy that G8 assistance and engagement were creating during the 1990s. Rather, it is rather a precarious power of enormous potential on the verge of a collapse which threatens the global system and the capacity of the G7/8 to cope.

Such dramatic shifts in relative capability and foreign policy orientation are in large part the result of powerful new processes now at work in the world. The proliferating speed, breadth and depth of international action by civil society actors and individuals are currently creating a new fully global system that demands continuous, comprehensive, effective global governance in response. The speed and accessibility of information and communication is evident in global financial markets, which countries wishing to preserve stable currencies or peculiar, opaque national financial systems can no longer easily resist.

With a few exceptions, most regions are now part of this single integrated global system, as the opening that came with the democratic-market revolution of the 1990s has now been reinforced by an often painful internationally-engaged re-orientation in foreign policy and a wrenching reform of domestic institutions and practices in support. Partly as a result, subjects long dealt with essentially or entirely as an essential part of domestic politics, and considered to be part of the hard core of a nation's sovereign prerogatives - the supervision of national banks and financial institutions, employment and employability programs for citizens, regulating direct investment and combatting crime - have now been elevated to the international level as the central agenda.

These transformations are giving the institutions of global governance, beginning with the G7/8, a new agenda, and forcing fast-paced processes of reform in an effort to cope. Thus financial supervision since the Halifax Summit of 1995, employment as a microeconomic focus since the Detroit ministerial of 1994 and crime since the Ottawa ministerial meeting of 1995 and the Lyon Summit of 1996 have become the centre of G7 concern. To address such issues, for example, transnational crime, it has been necessary to involve other countries and include Russia as a new member. A proliferating array of ministerial forums for a vast array of subjects have left leaders free to deal in depth with immediate crises and longer term priorities. The new Birmingham model for conducting the annual G7/G8 Summit, introduced by British Prime Minister Tony Blair in May 1998 and destined to be repeated by the German Chancellor as host of the 1999 Summit in June at Cologne, represents the most recent major attempt to make the G7/8 an effective centre of global governance for this new world.

The Analyses

To explore how these new critical global issues are being managed, the role of the reformed G7/G8 in this regard, and the potential of the G7/G8 as the effective centre of global governance in the transformed world of the new millennium, it is necessary to examine in turn when and why the G7/G8 performs as an effective international institution, how it is addressing its core task of managing the global financial and economic system, and how well it is coping with the newly globalized priorities of investment, employment and crime.

Thus Part I provides an overview of the recent performance of the G7/8 in fostering policy cooperation and coordination, compliance with collective commitments, and crisis management. It offers refined versions of the classic models of G7/8 performance and applies them to the contemporary G8 agenda and the new forces at work as the millennium approaches. It features three chapters written by the major theorists of G7 behaviour and a fourth chapter offering a critique of the argument that the G8 is becoming or should become a centre of global governance.

This examination begins, in Chapter 2, with Sir Nicholas Bayne's exploration of "Continuity and Leadership in an Age of Globalization". Here, the leading scholarly and practitioner analyst of the G7 points to the need for the G7/8 to deal persistently with the world's core problems, to expand its institutional capacity to this end and to focus on its unique advantages as an international institution. Contrary to initial hopes and claims, Bayne argues, the summits have not been good at forecasting trends (though they are good at crisis management), nor in choosing successful policies first time round.   But, to their credit, they keep returning to issues until they get them right. The focus at Birmingham on what are "the Four Horsemen of Globalization" - job loss, crime, financial panic and world poverty - is not new, as all four themes have recurred in various forms during the summit's history. To make an impact, the summits need to establish continuity; and that requirement is expanding the G7/G8 apparatus and making the summits themselves less distinct from other international methods.

In Chapter 3, on "Explaining G8 Effectiveness", John Kirton offers a more optimistic assessment of the G7's performance and potential, but one that points in the same direction toward the institutional adaptations required for the new millennium. Kirton argues that as the post cold war globalizing world of the 1990s moves into the new millennium, the G7 and new G8 are emerging as an effective centre, and are prospectively the effective centre of global governance.

During the 1990s the institution has enjoyed an enduring and enlarging success in forwarding, against formidable resistance, the new core values of inclusive democracy, ecologically sustainable market economies, and international openness and engagement. Its recent success and future potential rests on four foundations: the growing systemic predominance of capability and equality of capability within the G8; increasingly deep inter-dependence and intervulnerability among G8 members; a common commit-ment to the core values of market democracy, sustainable development, social equity and human rights; and the G8's unique operation by popularly and democratically elected leaders free of bureaucratic constraint.

In Chapter 4, on "The G8 and the New Political Economy", Michael Hodges offers a far more skeptical analysis. He suggests the capacity of the G7/8 to fulfill the hopes invested in it is limited. Its current membership makes little sense in the 21st century, after the Euro, expansion of the World Trade Organization (WTO) and the proliferation of other regional and mul-tilateral organizations. If Russia is included, should not China also be a member? It would make more sense to return to fireside chats for the US, Japan, the European Union (EU) Presidency and Commission, perhaps the European Central Bank (ECB) and leave concrete tasks to other, broader organizations. In that way the world could reap the unique advantage of the G7 as a deliberative, catalytic and direction setting forum, while leaving decision-making and implementation to other institutions with the multilat-eral membership and organizational capacity required.

The actual record of the G7 in collective decisionmaking and implementation is the focus of Chapter 5, where Ella Kokotsis and Joseph Daniels take a close look at "G8 Summits and Compliance". They note that since the inception of the summit, there has been little effort to analyze and explain compliance with summit commitments as a foundation for identify-ing proposals to improve the summit's compliance record. They report the results of the existing data on compliance with G7 commitments, identify the factors that create higher compliance in certain issue areas, and offer suggestions for improving the compliance record of the G7/G8 member states with their summit commitments.

Part II of this volume turns to the courses, causes, and challenges of contemporary G7/8 performance and its potential in regard to the core financial issues bred by intensified globalization. These include classic macroeconomic management, now centered in the reform of the Japanese economy, challenges to the international financial system in the light of the recent Asian-initiated crisis, the process of constructing a new international financial architecture, and the means to promote growth and monetary stability in the world economy.

In Chapter 6, on "**Japan's** Summit Contributions and Economic Challenges", Koji Watanabe argues that for Japan, the annual G7 summit - now G8 - has been, and still is, among the most important international forums for Japanese politics, not just diplomatically, but also for domestic politics. However, macroeconomic policy coordination - one of the key themes since the summit's inception - has had its limits in preventing the Japanese economy from moving from boom to bust in the late 80s and early 90s. One of the reasons might be that summit coordination has tended to be centered on external balance issues. The crucial issue for Japan now is how to deal with the trade-off between economic recovery and structural reform - an issue that the Japanese government failed to adequately handle in 1996-97.

In Chapter 7, "Supervising the International Financial System", Joseph Daniels examines the evolution and globalization of domestic financial systems. The problems and risks inherent in the system are discussed and the recent calls for global supervision and regulation considered. Daniels argues that the G8 and G7 have enjoyed limited successes and, more often than not, have failed to provide an effective leadership role in this issue area. Further, Daniels claims that existing institutions such as the International Monetary Fund (IMF), the World Bank, the Bank for International Settlements (BIS), and the Group of Ten (G10) lack the resources and ability to resolve or mitigate inevitable financial crises.

In Chapter 8, "Promoting Growth in the World Economy", Bronwyn Curtis examines the forces that have forced changes in the economies of the United States and the United Kingdom, and will force changes in the economies of continental Europe. She argues that competition, globalization, and monetary unification will force changes that otherwise would be politically unpalatable. Particularly in Europe, the constraints imposed by monetary unification and the forces of de-industrialization will bring about structural change in all the various sectors of the European economies.

In Chapter 9, on "Managing the Global Economy", Charles Goodhart discusses the opportunities for reform and policy action in light of the recent East Asian financial crises. Goodhart argues that rigidly fixed exchange rate regimes have proved too fragile for the developing and emerging economies and that financial reform would be needed before adopting a currency board arrangement. Goodhart also argues that financial reform is needed before full capital account liberalization can take place. Additionally he examines the IMF response to the recent crises, which, as he argues, was slow and perhaps inappropriate given the nature of the crises. Goodhart concludes with an interesting perspective on the winners and losers in the crises.

Part III of this volume moves from the financial core of the G7 and global agenda to deal with a broader array of priority issues. It explores how the G8 has coped with the new, once largely domestic or bilateral issues, which intensifying processes of deepening integration have now placed prominently on the international agenda. These include cases, notably investment, where the G7 has long been active but where its recent performance appears to many to be wanting. It also includes newer cases of G7/8 emphasis, such as employment and crime, where productive G7 action is more in evidence.

In Chapter 10, on "Negotiating Multilateral Rules to Promote Investment", Alan Rugman takes up a central issue in a world of deepening integration, in which foreign direct investment is increasing far faster than international trade and in which governments are struggling to create a global regime of rules to govern such investment, from their regional foundations in North America's NAFTA, Europe's European Union, and Asia's Asia-Pacific Economic Co-operation (APEC). Rugman argues that an important topic for the G8 should be how to rescue the Multilateral Agreement on Investment (MAI) from imminent failure. The design and adoption of a clear set of multilateral investment rules should be a priority for the G8 leaders. After exploring the reasons for the political failure of the MAI despite its economic benefits, the Canadian experience with the MAI is used to illustrate the negative side of non-governmental organizations (NGOs) in the MAI process.

In Chapter 11, on "Designing Effective Policies for Employment Creation", Richard Layard argues that the key to conquering unemployment

is to make individuals more employable - improving their appeal to employers and letting their wages adjust to reflect productivity.   Problems of
employment will not be solved through artificial rationing of work, nor
through exposing workers to unrestricted "hire and fire" practices. Progress
lies along a middle way between the unregulated labour markets of North
America and the overprotected system in Europe.

In Chapter 12, on "Combating Transnational Financial Crime"
George Staple takes a close look at how the proliferating problem of financial crime is countered by the existing international legal regime and by the
government of the world's largest financial centre, Britain. He highlights the
mismatch in a world where money can flow freely on an illegal as well as
legal basis, but where the criminal law and capacity to combat it remain
nationally based and supported only by very limited international cooperation. In the face of large scale international fraud, the British Government
has moved to institute new protective measures nationally, within the
European Union, and through the G8. Yet, while Britain offers enhanced
assistance to foreign governments conducting international investigations
and trials in Britain, there is a need for new international action to facilitate
these processes and the assistance Britain needs from foreign governments
when pursuing criminals abroad. Moreover, despite G8 action beginning in
1988 and the May 1998 G8 decision to expand the Financial Action Task
Force (FATF), there are further measures needed to counter the burgeoning
transnational crime of money laundering.   Notwithstanding impressive
national and European initiatives, Staple concludes, much more could be
done, through G8 leadership, at the international level.

Conclusions

As is evident from these chapters, this volume offers a vibrant and diverse
array of views about the proper role of the G7/8, the causes of past success,
the adequacy of its current reforms, the management of pressing issues, and
prescriptions for future action and institutional adjustment. This richness in
analysis reflects the initial conviction that understanding the world of the new
millennium and the G7/8's role in governing it would be best secured not by
imposing a single perspective but by allowing for an open ended and far-
reaching probe into past performance and a largely unknown emerging
future. Thus these analyses began united only in the conviction that the
world of the new millennium could well be different in several important

respects from even the recent past and that the G7/8 was worthy of more intense and critical scrutiny as an institution that could have an substantial role in governing it. Yet beyond these initial premises, and amidst the rich diversity of analysis, argument and advocacy, some common themes emerge.

Current Performance

There is a widespread view that the G7/8 has exhibited a widely varying performance over time and across issue areas - that it has been and can be effective, even though its actual performance of late has often been highly disappointing. The most optimistic assessment comes from John Kirton, who argues that the decade of the 1990s has seen the G7/8 return to the high performance of its early years, and that its consistently strong record means it is poised to emerge as the centre of global governance in the new millennium. A shared if more sober view comes from Kokotsis and Daniels who see the summit making ambitious specific commitments that are complied with in the environment, development and even economic fields. It is thus worth having as a governance mechanism in the international community. Bayne too sees the summit as effective, if not on its first encounter with an issue but eventually as it perseveres to get matters right.

Many others see the G7 as being effective on specific issues at particular times. For Bayne it is in the management of acute crises that the summit excels. For Watanabe it is picking up new issues at an early stage, and in dealing with the Russian issue. Daniels sees the summit taking several well placed initiatives and actions in response to financial risks. For Staple, the G8 decision to expand the FATF to prompt anti-money laundering bodies to be established in broader areas of the world is a commendable step forward.

Yet these occasional successes are matched by a similar number of failures. Bayne asserts that the summit is no better than anyone else in forecasting crises. Watanabe suggests the G7 failed to warn of the possibility of a bust when Japan was basking in asset inflation. And for Daniels, by not handling effectively the present financial crisis, the G8 has demonstrated that it is not an institution of effective global leadership in the area of deepest importance.

Daniels' charge also points to the view that the G7/8 has been an overall failure. Indeed, Daniels concludes that the G7, the G8, and the summit process has not dealt effectively with the most pressing economic issue of 1998 - the fast-developing liquidity crisis of domestic financial sectors. The most pessimistic assessment comes from Hodges, who argues that repeated G7 failures, for example in multilateral trade liberalization, demonstrate that is not at all capable as serving as a centre of global governance.

Proper Role

In part these varying assessments of the G7/8's performance reflect different conceptions of the proper role the G7/8 does and should play in the global community. The most limited conception of its appropriate functions comes from Michael Hodges. He sees its utility as a club through which leaders of major powers bond with each other, raise consciousness about new issues, set an agenda, spin off initiatives, create networks, prod other institutions to do things, and assist in creating institutions that are suited to a particular task.

Others add additional or more specific functions. Bayne implies that it should also, despite past failures, anticipate and act to prevent crises before they become acute. For Daniels, it has a unique role in the reform of international financial institutions, particularly in bailouts of future financial crises, responsible IMF governance, review of the very need for the IMF and World Bank, and the design of approaches to supervisory coordination. Rugman adds the task of designing and adopting a clear set of multilateral investment rules. Layard feels employment is suitable for the G8 as a central theme. Staple asserts the G8 should provide leadership in securing international cooperation on transnational crime.

Causes of Success and Failure

These varying conceptions of the G7/8's performance and proper role depend on, and point to, different factors that generate success. Here, the major theorists of summit success offer enhanced versions of their familiar theories, while the other authors offer important additions.

Among the traditional theorists, Bayne goes beyond the classic Putnam-Bayne emphasis on American leadership, lessons of the past and domestic coalition support to stress the role of sustained and interactive treatment of recurrent problems. Kirton affirms the importance of concerted power, constricted participation, common principles, and political control by popularly elected leaders (see also Hormats, 1998). But he modifies his former concert equality model by now pointing to constricted participation that allows for the association of outsiders, intensifying interdependence activated by crisis, common problems as well as principles, and multi-level political control involving ministers as well as leaders.   Kokotsis and Daniels continue to emphasize institutional variables at the national and international level and, along with Kirton, political control, but now give greater prominence to the expansion of both the preparatory and follow-up phases of the summits.

Among the other authors, Koji Watanabe argues that an effective multilateral surveillance system that allows members to share sufficient knowledge of the political as well as economic dynamics of the country concerned is a requisite for effective G7 macroeconomic policy coordination. Also important is a necessary focus on economic policy issues that are more relevant to external balances, and the psychology of popular and market optimism and pessimism that can render the effect of political messages emanating from the summit perverse.   Daniels sees failure arising when the G7 delegates to international organizations, such as the IMF, that are ill-equipped to deal with particular issues. Hodges too stresses the centrality of international organizational capacity, with the assured budgets, secretariats, permanent employees, continuous informal interactions, and well-tailored expertise they contain.

Proposals for Reform

These assessments of performance, proper roles, and causes of success and failure underlie and inspire various suggestions for G7/8 reform. Together the list of proposed reforms offered by the authors covers the full array of traditional dimensions, from membership and agenda to the degree and form of institutionalization (Merlini, 1994). Yet they also raise new issues - such as the engagement of civil society and the use of new technologies. They also show that the innovations of the Birmingham models are largely endorsed, but not fully embraced. The debate on G7/8 reform is thus sure to continue.

On the perennial question of membership, Hodges proposes that outside guests be invited on an ad hoc basis, in order to alleviate the sense of exclusion and enhance the legitimacy of the G7/8. He further suggests that the G8 create a formalized link with China, given the latter's growing importance to the world economy.

The question of the appropriate G7/8 agenda is the subject of differing views. Hodges proposes a focus on special themes and topics, as at Birmingham in 1998, but warns of the dangers of concentrating on too little. Kokotsis and Daniels, with a view to improving members' compliance with G7/8 commitments, present several specific suggestions about the agenda. They agree with Hodges on the need for less overload and greater focus on issues where the G7 can make a difference - on domestic policy issues where synergy with their internationalized equivalents can be achieved; where means-ends relationships are well understood and accepted; where leaders exercise real as well as formal authority; and where adequate domestic institutions exist for implementation.

There is also a lively debate on the institutionalization of the summit. Bayne, once cautious, now approves the extension of the lower-level G8 apparatus, in ways that make it easier for leaders to delegate. Kokotsis and Daniels, raising doubts about Birmingham's innovative leaders-only format, note that compliance is more likely to come if the ministers are in attendance on site. Hodges favours informality, suggesting the summit process, as at Birmingham, should let leaders retreat to an isolated country home to discuss what they want by themselves. Goodhart raises the issue of institutionalization and automaticity at the domestic level, wondering if members would be prepared to put in their bond covenants clauses that would automatically convert fixed interest rates into equity when financial crisis looms.

Bayne raises two newer issues of summit reform. He argues that the G8 should mobilize its democratic legitimacy by looking beyond government, particularly by forging better links to the private business community. He further proposes that the G7/8 make better use of Internet-related technology to argue for the benefits of globalization and respond to the anxieties about it that the public in member countries have.

Despite these differences, none of the authors takes issue with the basic presumption that the new millennium will bring not just a new century in a chronological sense but also, and far more importantly, a transformed real world. And despite often severe criticisms of the G7/8's recent performance and current configuration, none suggest that it should retreat from the challenge of providing leadership in managing the transition into this new world. In that particular sense, all concur that the G7/8 can become an effective center of global governance as the new millennium dawns.

References

Bergsten, F.C. (1998), "The Great War: The Euro vs. The Dollar", *The International Economy*, (May/June), pp. 8.

Bergsten, F. and Henning, C.R. (1996), *Global Economic Leadership and the Group of Seven*, Institute for International Economics, Washington, D.C.

Hale, D. (1998), "What the Asian Crisis Is All About", *The International Economy*, (January/February), pp. 18-23.

Hormats, R.D. (1998), "Commanding Thoughts", *The International Economy*, (January/February), pp. 44-45 & 62.

Ikenberry, J. (1993), "Salvaging the G-7", *Foreign Affairs* 72 (Spring), pp. 132-139.

Kirton, J. (1989), "The Seven Power Summit as an International Concert", Paper presented at the International Studies Association Annual meeting, London, England, April.

Kirton, J. (1993), "The Seven Power Summit and the New Security Agenda", In D. Dewitt, D. Haglund and J. Kirton, eds., *Building a New Global Order: Emerging Trends in International Security*, Oxford University Press, Toronto, pp. 335-357.

Kokotsis, E. (1998), *National Compliance with G7 Environment and Development Commitments, 1975-1995*, Ph.D. Thesis, University of Toronto (January).

Kokotsis, E. and Kirton, J. (1997), "National Compliance with Environmental Regimes: The Case of the G7, 1988-1995", Paper prepared for the Annual Convention of the International Studies Association, Toronto, March 18-22.

Malmgren, H. B. (1998), "Dark Clouds Over Russia?", *The International Economy*, (January/February), pp. 30-33.

Merlini, C. (ed) (1994), "The Future of the G-7 Summits", *The International Spectator* 29 (April-June).

Mulford, D. (1998), "Mulford Memorandum", *The International Economy*, (January/February), pp. 10-13 & 60.

Putnam, R. and Bayne, N. (1987), *Hanging Together: The Seven Power Summits*, Harvard University Press, Cambridge, Mass.

Wallace, W. (1984), "Political Issues at the Summits: A New Concert of Powers?", in C. Merlini (ed), *Economic Summits and Western Decision-Making*, Croom Helm, London & Sydney.

Part I
Explaining G8 Effectiveness

2 Continuity and Leadership in an Age of Globalisation

NICHOLAS BAYNE

Introduction

I have been researching and writing about the summits for 16 years now, more than half their lifetime.[1] Vicariously - if not in reality - I have accompanied the leaders as they scaled all the summits since 1975. The experience is itself rather like climbing a mountain. The higher one goes, the further one can see, so that the vantage appears quite differently from a new angle. In particular, what looked like isolated peaks from lower down reveal themselves as all part of the same range.

Continuity and iteration at the summits, rather than their individual outcomes, is fundamental to the summits and their success.[2] Each summit is presented as a new event, confronting fresh challenges and marking fresh achievements. Each summit host naturally tries to build up this impression of innovation and originality. But the greatest contribution of the summits is their sustained and iterative treatment of recurrent problems, which reappear time and time again.

This chapter examines the record of the summits in this light. The first part explains how and why the summit keeps on returning to problems. The second part illustrates this in relation to the themes chosen for the 1998 Birmingham summit. These themes reflect present anxieties about globalisation but also have much deeper roots. The third part looks at the institutional consequences. It draws from this analysis and the experience of the first summit where leaders were meeting alone the conclusions that summits are successful through their continuity and iteration, and that the emergence of a lower level Group of Eight (G8) apparatus will reinforce this effectiveness. However, the summits need to better involve the private sector and use the new communications technologies to make the case for the benefits of globalisation.

Continuity and Iteration at the Summits

Summits were originally intended, especially by French President Giscard and his European colleagues, to be single free-standing events. The leaders would gather to address a set of problems that had defied solution at lower levels. Their leadership qualities would enable them to reach solutions: leadership as heads of government, with supreme responsibility; and leadership as representing the most powerful economies, whose joint decisions would be accepted by others. Having reached their conclusions, the leaders would disperse, to be called together when another set of intractable problems required their attention.

Of course, the summits very soon became an annual series. This was because the Europeans went along with the parallel American concept of the summit giving regular and systematic impulses to other international bodies. It did not mean the Group of Seven (G7) members had changed their view about their own leadership qualities. To this day, the leaders expect to reach agreements or achieve results that have eluded their minister's at lower levels - or else why should they meet at all?

One abiding vision of the summit, which remains prevalent in the late 1990s, is that the summits should make their unique contribution each year by providing leadership and agreed decisions, and then hand on their recommendations to be pursued by their cabinet colleagues or, more often, the competent international institutions. With this model the leaders only intervene at the point where they are needed. Their agenda need not become cluttered as issues move off it to make way for new ones. Preparations would be organised by a light, un-bureaucratic structure of personal representatives. This vision still exercises a strong attraction, not least on the leaders themselves.[3]

There have been times, especially in the early years, when the summits did operate like this; where issues came to the summit for one or two years and were then entrusted to wider international bodies and did not recur at the summit level. The international monetary system was the central theme for Rambouillet 1975, but it did not come back to the summit again for many years thereafter. Energy issues, central in 1979 and 1980, have not required the same attention since.

In more recent years, the summit concentrated on mobilising help for Central European countries in 1989 and 1990, but then switched its attention to Russia. The summit's review of international institutions, launched at Naples 1994, was in itself an iterative process. However, it can also be interpreted as a strategy to make these institutions better equipped to handle recommendations from the summits and thereby take pressure off the summits themselves.

These are, however, isolated episodes in summit history. The usual pattern is of continuity and iteration. The summits come back and back to the same issues, seldom being able to clear them off their agenda altogether. It is necessary to examine the reasons why this happens. Four main reasons can be identified: perseverance with difficult problems; dealing with new and unexpected issues; institutional inadequacy; and the consequences of globalisation.

Perseverance with Difficult Problems

A few issues became recurrent features on the summit agenda because they were thought to deserve the attention of the leaders every year. Macro-economic policy coordination was such an issue in the early years, though it is now largely delegated to finance ministers. International trade issues always concern the leaders in some form. While trade negotiations are in progress, as with the Tokyo Round in 1975-79 or the Uruguay Round in 1986-93, the summit encourages them to reach a successful conclusion. In between global rounds, the summit seeks to prevent protectionist trends from regaining ground.

More importantly, many issues keep coming back to the summit because the leaders failed to reach the right solution on their first attempt. The problems that come to the summit are inherently very difficult. If they had been easy, they would have been solved at lower levels. It is no surprise, and no reproach to the summits, if they do not get them right the first time. But the leaders do not give up and declare it all too difficult. They keep at it, returning again and again to intractable issues until they have agreed on an effective and acceptable outcome. It is to the credit of the leaders, and of the summit as an institution, that they keep on trying, despite the public criticism provoked by their lack of initial success.

This persistence is a dominant feature of summit history. There are many examples of it. It happened with both the Tokyo and the Uruguay Rounds of trade negotiations. The summits set deadlines for their completion, but then failed to honour these commitments because of disagreements among G7 members. But despite this, and in the face of much criticism, the leaders persevered and did finally succeed in bringing the two trade rounds to their desired conclusion in 1979 and 1993. The summits' dealings with Russia show a similar sequence. It took three years, from 1991 to 1993, before they established a satisfactory framework for providing help to the Russian economy; and another five years, from 1994 to 1998, to resolve the exact relationship of Russia with the summit. This process ended with 1998's official conversion of the summit from G7 to G8. Other examples are examined below.

New and Unexpected Issues

Summits aim to be innovative. They identify new issues of concern to the world community and stimulate new forms of international action. But it takes time to change people's thinking and develop new policies. Thus the summits from 1989 to 1991 stimulated innovative thinking on global environmental issues in the run-up to the Rio Environment Conference, breaking new ground. During the same period they acted as pioneers in the international treatment of terrorism and drug smuggling, addressing new issues each year.

The summits have a good record in crisis management once the crisis has broken. But they are no better than anyone else at forecasting crises. Their record at predicting financial upheavals is especially poor. The summits did not anticipate the turmoil in Latin America in 1982, in Mexico in 1994 or in East Asia in 1997. When leaders are taken by surprise in this way they have to come back to the issues in question, as they have done with debt and financial instability.

Institutional Inadequacy

The recurrence of issues at the summit is affected by the quality and the varying levels of coverage provided by the international institutions to which the leaders can pass on issues for further treatment. Recommendations on trade and financial issues can be passed on readily to the General Agreement on Tariffs and Trade (GATT) or World Trade Organisation (WTO), the International Monetary Fund (IMF) or the World Bank. But in other areas, the institutions are fragmented, as in regards to the global environment, or largely unsatisfactory, as with international crime. So the summits have to return to these issues themselves and create their own apparatus for follow-up in order to maintain any progress.

The Consequences of Globalisation

One major consequence of globalisation is a direct cause of iteration at the summits. Globalisation progressively limits the policy instruments in the hands of G8 governments, particularly instruments of short-term impact. Monetary policy is now largely in the hands of independent central banks. Fiscal policy is set in a long-term context and is rarely used for immediate macro-economic impact. Many policies, formerly in the hands of government, have now moved to the private sector.

Most of the economic levers still available to governments are not quick-acting. They only make an impact over time. This means that issues may need several years of summit treatment before any change is visible. The summits at Naples in 1994 and Lyon in 1996 already focused on employment issues. But because the improvement in employment levels was slow to appear, the subject came back onto the agenda for Birmingham. From this analysis some preliminary conclusions can be drawn. The summits do not achieve results by flashes of prescient, inspirational decision-making, sparked by the personal chemistry between the leaders. There are a few examples of this, but they are very rare. Nor do they often achieve, at the first attempt, a definitive settlement of issues which can then be handed on to other institutions. Nearly always their achievement comes from dogged persistence, a sort of "worrying away" at the issues until they have reached a solution.

One operational consequence of this recurrent treatment of issues at the summit is constant pressure on the agenda. More and more issues demand treatment by the leaders, but few can be put away as definitely solved. Overloading, which had always threatened the summits, came to a head in the early 1990s. A rebellion launched by British Prime Minister Major generated a sustained effort to organise the leaders' time better and to allow them more spontaneous debate, rather than being swamped by paper. This led to the summit meeting in 1998 taking place, for the first time ever, among leaders only without supporting ministers.

But this apparent lightening is deceptive. The foreign and finance ministers are still meeting, but separately, a week before the heads of government. In 1998 they met in four different combinations: G7 finance; G8 finance; G8 foreign; and G8 foreign and finance ministers jointly. They issued over 40 pages of agreed documentation plus national employment plans for each participant. The number of issues tackled by the G8 does not diminish and the G8 apparatus continues to proliferate.

Issues for Birmingham: The Four Horsemen of Globalisation

The Birmingham summit was the first of the series to be consecrated wholly to the fears and anxieties generated by globalisation. Earlier summits of the 1990s, from Naples 1994 onwards, recognised globalisation as a powerful, all-embracing force, with benefits as well as dangers. Recognition of this force provided the context for the leaders' decisions. The first response of the leaders to globalisation was to conduct a review of international institutions, to see if they could stand up to the new pressures put upon them and to propose reforms to make them more effective.[4] This process occupied the leaders at Halifax in 1995, Lyon in 1996 and Denver in 1997, after which the initial impetus was then exhausted. The leaders at Birmingham addressed popular anxieties about globalisation directly. They chose an agenda consisting of four issues that worried their respective electorates deeply about globalisation. These were: job loss; cross-border crime; financial panic; and world poverty.

Globalisation presents G8 governments with a dilemma. They know the removal of barriers to economic activity, leading to greater competition, together with access to new technology, is the cause of their growing prosperity. Governments have acted upon this conviction, by getting out of the way of economic competition, renouncing various powers and transferring large chunks of former government business, like public utilities, to the private sector.

But globalisation disturbs the very people upon whom the power of democratic governments depend. The people see the darker side of globalisation and feel vulnerable to external pressures over which they have no control. They worry that their jobs are threatened, that crime is rising, that financial markets behave irrationally and that the poorest are neglected both at home and in the world at large. They expect their governments to do something about these worries. Governments in turn want to respond, but even where they have the power they often cannot protect their people from the risks of globalisation without forfeiting its benefits.

That is why the advance of globalisation brings issues back to the fore of public consciousness and back onto the summit agenda. Of the three themes for Birmingham, employment and crime were specific initiatives launched at the Denver summit the year before. Global economic issues, the third more general theme, inevitably came to focus on the Asian financial crisis, though it also looked more widely at the problems of the world's poorest countries, especially their debt burdens. All these themes go right back to the origins of the G7 and have recurred at the summit over the years. However, globalisation adds a new dimension to each of them.

The analysis that follows concentrates on the persistence of these problems and the sustained determination of the summits to tackle them, rather than on the solutions which emerged from Birmingham. None were settled definitively in 1998. All are likely to need iterative treatment, with more attention at future summits.

The First Horseman: Job Loss

Birmingham was the third summit in five years to address unemployment. It followed a standard model for G7/G8 discussions: a preparatory meeting of finance and employment ministers early in the year was followed by summit treatment later. This model was launched in 1994, with the Detroit ministerial that preceded Naples; repeated in 1996 by the Lille conference before Lyon; and repeated again by the London meeting of February 1998 to prepare for Birmingham. At Naples and Lyon the leaders in fact added little to what their ministers had concluded. Neither summit can claim to have had a sustained impact on employment levels. Economic conditions became easier, but even so, the leaders at Birmingham did little more than add their authority to their ministers' work.

Detailed discussions of employment-promoting measures, as in 1994, 1996 and 1998, are new to the G7/G8. They reflect the leaders' reaction to their people's fear that globalisation destroys jobs. The participating governments hope to develop "best practice" among themselves and to learn from each others' experience, good or bad. Employment measures of this kind remain largely domestic policies, even in the European Union (EU).

Employment has, however, been on the summit agenda in some form from the very start. The debate has moved a very long way over the years. The early summits concentrated on two arguments: whether macro-economic policy should tolerate inflation to sustain jobs; and whether trade protection was justified to preserve jobs.

The first argument was settled very early on. Despite pressure from the British government of the day, the summits had decided by 1977 that there was no trade-off between inflation and unemployment. The 1977 London summit declaration said bluntly: "Inflation does not reduce unemployment; on the contrary, it is one of its major causes". The priority given to fighting inflation through macro-economic policy has risen steadily over the 20 subsequent years. The European experience of the 1980s and 1990s has also shown that once a recession has caused the loss of jobs, renewed growth on its own is not enough to restore them. So G7/G8 governments, following the advice of the Organisation for Economic Co-operation and Development (OECD), have come to focus on the micro-economic, structural measures that were on the table at Birmingham.[5]

In the second argument, those advocating trade protection to save jobs have been kept in check. But the struggle has been fierce and is still not resolved. At Rambouillet in 1975 the other leaders denied British Prime Minister Wilson the right to keep out imports to protect threatened industries. From 1975-79 and again from 1986-93, the summits insisted on a successful outcome from the GATT multilateral trade negotiations - even when they could not deliver - because this was the best way of keeping protectionist pressures in check at home. In the interval between the two GATT rounds the rise of the US dollar and transatlantic disputes over launching the Uruguay Round (especially at the 1985 Bonn summit) enabled protectionist ideas to make dangerous advances in the United States. Checking protectionism was thus the motive behind US Treasury Secretary Baker's initiative for the Plaza Agreement of September 1985, so that a lower dollar would restore the competitive position of US industry.

Since the Uruguay Round ended five years ago, the advance of globalisation has produced a new range of arguments in favour of protectionism. These arguments have attracted increased political support, so that by 1997 US President Clinton did not dare to table legislation to give his Administration "fast-track" authority in future trade negotiations for fear it might not carry. The Asian financial crisis will increase the controversy. As the Asian economies, with much weaker currencies, seek to export their way back to strong economic growth, the trade balances in the US, Europe and Japan will have to take the strain and Western industry will feel exposed to a new wave of Asian competition.[6]

Trade, employment and protectionism are fundamental issues for the G8. The leaders are better able to argue the case for free trade and open markets if they are actively working together to improve employment conditions by other measures. That is the underlying value of the exchanges on employment at the summit of the last five years. That is also why the summit leaders will keep returning to this subject, even if the benefits are slow to appear.

The Second Horseman: Cross-border Crime

Birmingham is the first summit where crime was chosen as a principal theme. This was not, however, a sudden appearance of the subject. In the preparations for Halifax in 1995, crime was identified as a theme for treatment in the review of global institutions. Serious work on crime began in the preparations for Lyon 1996, though this was diverted at the summit to serve US short-term concerns about terrorism following a terrorist attack on American servicemen in Saudi Arabia. More expert work was also done for Denver 1997. But the leaders there felt the issue needed higher priority and agreed to focus on it at Birmingham.

In all the G8 countries there is a growing fear of crime, especially violent crime and fraud, even where the actual crime figures do not justify it. Globalisation alone does not create this fear, which has more complex causes. But it feeds the fear. The speed of communications and the openness of borders and markets, which enhance life for the honest citizen, make conditions easier for the criminal too. In some countries, organised crime can even undermine the fabric of the state. Russia is especially vulnerable, having moved abruptly from an authoritarian society to an open market and democratic structures without much prior experience of either. The presence of Russia in the G8 gives added impetus to the summit's work on crime.

International public order issues of this kind in fact go back to the roots of summitry. Terrorism and aircraft hijacking were the first non-economic issues to be taken up at the summits. German Chancellor Schmidt raised hijacking spontaneously at Bonn in 1978 and the leaders adopted a decision on the spot - one of the rare examples of summit inspiration. Terrorism, with hostage-taking, preoccupied the summits of the early 1980s. It was the major political issue for Tokyo 1986, which agreed on a common position on state-sponsored terrorism, ending divisions among the G7 after the US bombing raid on Libya.

Drugs likewise first came onto the G7 agenda spontaneously, being raised by US President Reagan and British Prime Minister Thatcher at Bonn 1985. From 1989 onwards, the summits went deeply into various aspects of illicit drug smuggling. The Paris Arch summit of 1989, for example, set up the Financial Action Task Force (FATF) to check the laundering of drug money. The FATF is still very much in operation. The end of the Cold War has had a perverse effect on this subject. More open frontiers make it easier to move illicit drugs from centres of production in Asia to consumers in Europe, both East and West. New fears also arise of the smuggling of nuclear material from the abandoned Russian stockpiles, which could put weapons of mass destruction into unauthorised hands.

Previous summits have had varying success with these issues. Hijacking has largely disappeared. Tough, united policies on terrorism have reduced the incidence of international terrorist attacks, but they remain a danger, especially in the Middle East. Despite many years of effort, the damage done by illicit drugs seems undiminished and measures against money-laundering seem as necessary as ever.

Terrorism, drug trafficking, money laundering and nuclear smuggling are all examples of international crime encouraged or facilitated by more open systems and the easier movement of both people and finance - in short, by globalisation. But globalisation keeps adding new crimes to the international agenda, such as hi-tech crime and the smuggling of people and firearms. All were on the list for Birmingham.[7]

One major problem is the fragmentation and inadequacy of international institutions in this field. Traditionally the interior and justice ministries responsible for fighting crime have not been internationally minded. The G7 and G8 now have well-established practices of cooperation. Expert groups on terrorism and drugs have been meeting since the mid-1980s. These have been reinforced since 1995 by the Lyon Group, with a wider agenda, and by G8 ministerial meetings. Even among the G8, it is proving easier to cooperate in catching criminals than in ensuring their conviction.

Beyond the G8, global institutions need to be strengthened and given wider powers to enforce agreed international disciplines. The United Nations (UN) can draw up international conventions containing strong commitments, but it has no power to ensure compliance. It cannot oblige its members to amend their judicial systems and remove the barriers behind which international criminals can hide. The UN's drug program also needs better organisation and more resources. Rather than encouraging yet more action at G8 level, the task after Birmingham is to build stronger worldwide institutions to check cross-border crime. This will require a sustained campaign before the G8 can take crime off their agenda again.

The Third Horseman: Financial Panic

Birmingham was obliged to consider the impact of the Asian financial crisis of 1997-98 and its implications for the IMF and World Bank. This was not part of the plan. Only three years ago, in the light of the Mexican crisis of 1994-95, the Halifax summit addressed the reform of the Fund and the Bank as part of the institutional review. The summit endorsed a substantial reform program prepared by the G7 finance ministers, which was adopted by the Fund and the Bank collectively and without difficulty. The whole operation appeared effective and harmonious.

Even in 1995, this did not look like the summit's last word on financial crises, the IMF and the World Bank. One weakness was visible from the start. The IMF adopted stricter standards on the supply of economic and financial data to give clearer warnings of any impending crises. But countries under threat had the strongest incentive to conceal the true figures, especially at times of political uncertainty, like elections. Events showed that in 1997 Korea, Thailand and Indonesia all concealed the full extent of their financial exposure, making the crisis much worse when it did finally overtake them.

No one expected another financial panic would follow so soon after the Mexican crisis. This time more countries were affected and the consequences were worse. For Korea, Thailand and Indonesia, and even some other Asian countries, it is arguable that they were suffering because of their own mistakes. But far more countries have endured the loss of growth, capital outflows, currency and stockmarket collapses through no fault of their own. This appears to be one of the greatest dangers of globalisation: a volatile, unpredictable financial system, where money moves abruptly and on impulse, and penalises countries whose economic policies are sound as well as those who may deserve it.

When Canadian Prime Minister Chrétien decided that Halifax 1995 would focus on money and finance, he was harking back to the reason why Giscard convened the very first summit twenty years before: to put some "viscosity" into the world financial system. So this issue too goes back to the dawn of summitry.

In fact, Giscard had to acquiesce at Rambouillet 1975 to a regime of generalised floating which was endorsed by the IMF shortly thereafter. He obtained only a limited undertaking by the G7 to intervene "to counter disorderly conditions" in the exchange markets. In practice, G7 currencies continued to fluctuate against each other, because of divergent economic policies rather than "disorderly conditions". These fluctuations were not initially a brake on growth as long as the expansion of private bank lending "recycled" the surpluses of the oil producers.

All this was upset by the world recession of 1981-82, following the second oil shock, and by policies introduced by the Reagan Administration, which began to drive up the dollar. At Versailles in 1982 the G7 leaders agreed among themselves on a system of mutual surveillance of economic policies, to reduce the risk of currency fluctuations.   This was greatly enhanced following the Plaza Agreement of 1985 and has become a standing activity of the G7 finance ministers, while gradually passing out of the ambit of the heads of government.   Outsiders tend to find the results of this process disappointing; but the practising governments value it.[8]

At Versailles 1982 the G7 had focused on their own problems, not on the world at large.   Only a few weeks later Mexico, Brazil and Argentina threatened to default on their debts, which they had accumulated by recycling and could no longer service.   This brought international financial issues back onto the summit agenda in a different form, where they recurred over several years, until a solution was found.   Multi-year rescheduling agreements, endorsed at London in 1984, did not suffice; nor did the additional lending provided by the "Baker Plan" of 1985.   These debt problems were finally resolved by writing down the debts below their nominal value under the "Brady Plan" that was endorsed at the Paris Arch summit of 1989. The Brady Plan proved very effective for the problem it addressed.   But solving one problem only exposed two new ones.

The first problem arose because the financial markets open to middle-income countries have been transformed.   Banks have become more cautious over sovereign lending; but countries in search of finance can tap a much wider range of sources, often from institutions much less closely supervised than the banks.   So the crises which affected Mexico in 1994 and the three Asian countries in 1997 were harder to predict, spread much further and faster, and required an urgent and massive mobilisation of resources to bring them under control.   The IMF, World Bank and supporting governments had to commit a total of $112 billion to check the Asian financial crisis.[9]

The Fourth Horseman: World Poverty

The second problem may be less serious for the world economy, but it is worse in human terms: the mounting debt burden of low-income countries. This problem reveals the fourth horseman - the risks of globalisation for the poorest.   Mexico, Korea, Thailand and Indonesia, despite their recent troubles, have benefited greatly over the years from globalisation.   They have achieved rapid growth rates and attracted large amounts of valuable foreign investment.   But many low-income countries have been in no position to make gains from globalisation.   With some notable exceptions, low-income countries, especially in Africa, have fallen even further behind as a result of globalisation, while the middle-income countries close the gap on the mature economies. Often the low-income countries fall behind because of their own policy mistakes. But their poverty makes them ill-placed to compete in world markets or to attract private foreign investment.

The summits have had relations with developing countries on their agenda from the start, but without making any impact on the problems of the poorest for many years. The first serious contribution came with the 1988 Toronto summit, which endorsed proposals for debt relief for low-income countries pursuing reforms agreed to with the IMF. These proposals offered relief equivalent to one-third of debts owed to the creditor governments grouped in the Paris Club. They were adopted by the IMF and the Paris Club and were known as the "Toronto terms".

As usual, the summit needed several attempts at this subject. Toronto terms proved inadequate for many low-income debtors, despite good records with the IMF. An improved version, called the "Trinidad terms", was first launched by Britain at the Commonwealth finance ministers meeting in 1990. After long argument, these terms were agreed to by all the G7 at Naples 1994 and likewise adopted by the IMF and the Paris Club. Trinidad terms became Naples terms, with relief of up to two-thirds of Paris Club debt.

But Trinidad terms did not provide relief on debts owed to the Fund and Bank themselves, which were often the largest component of these countries' debt. Another British initiative in the Commonwealth led to the Highly-Indebted Poor Countries (HIPC) debt relief program, supported by the IMF and World Bank and endorsed by the G7 at Lyon 1996. This combines up to 80% relief from the Paris Club with additional lending from the IMF and World Bank, to set against their earlier loans. Up to 41 poor countries could benefit from this. But implementation is very slow and deserving poor countries suffer while waiting. In consequence, the Commonwealth in 1997 endorsed a third British proposal, the Mauritius Mandate, intended to speed things up.

Debt is not the only problem affecting low-income countries, nor the only one addressed by recent summits, which have given more attention than their predecessors to issues concerning the poorest. Lyon 1996 looked at development policies generally and the reform of development institutions. Denver 1997 focused on Africa, as the Clinton Administration was introducing new African policies. The British government also wanted Birmingham to focus on the problems of low-income countries, despite having to shift attention to the Asian financial crisis.

This renewed attention is welcome. But the results so far are disappointing. Recent summit declarations have been full of good advice and exhortation. But they have been short on precise commitments, except on debt. Neither what is said on trade opportunities for low-income countries nor on future aid volumes provide much encouragement. Most G7 Governments that have squeezed their public spending to reduce budget deficits and passed more responsibility to the private sector find themselves unable to make exceptions for aid programmes.[10] They urge developing countries to take advantage of private sector funds and markets. But this advice is more useful for middle-income countries, with one foot already on the ladder, than for poor ones at the bottom and falling further behind. There is a glaring contrast between the $112 billion found to rescue Korea, Thailand and Indonesia and the limited aid and debt relief on offer for the poorest countries.[11]

Birmingham therefore confronted these two dangers of globalisation; one acute and episodic, one chronic. Creating a new international financial architecture and strengthening its institutions after the Asian crisis had already been the main theme for the IMF and International Bank for Reconstruction and Development (IBRD) meetings in Washington in April 1998. There were plenty of ideas for the heads to discuss; they took the lead from their finance ministers, adding little of their own. The measures include: better rules for financial supervision; even stronger disciplines on supplying correct economic data; the prospect of public rebukes from the IMF to those taking undue risks; better coordination between the Fund and Bank.

But, as after Halifax 1995, this will hardly be the last word. Even with these improved precautions, outbreaks of financial panic must be expected to recur in future. The huge amounts of money circulating in the system, combined with the herd instinct of the markets, can produce reversals of confidence of a scale and suddenness which far exceed the capacity of monetary authorities to control them. The markets themselves are constantly changing, with even faster communications and new financial instruments to meet new needs. So it is all too likely that financial panic and financial reform will come back to the G8 agenda again.

Poverty in low-income countries does not directly affect the economies of the G8, as unemployment, crime and financial panic do. Nor is it a preoccupation of the electorate as a whole. But it does concern a wide range of articulate and well-informed non-governmental organisations

(NGOs). As a result, the perceived failure of the G8 summits to do enough for the poorest developing countries is one of the strongest criticism leveled at the summits and the subject of popular demonstrations. At Birmingham, there was a march of 50-70,000 demonstrators around the summit site, urging the leaders to "break the chains of debt" and make the HIPC program faster and more generous.

The leaders did discuss this issue and made some moves forward, adopting part although not all of the Mauritius Mandate. They accepted the target date of 2000 for getting all eligible countries into the program. They made some guarded commitments on providing enough debt relief and on special help for "poor post-conflict countries". But this left more work to be done to speed up the process; the NGOs behind the demonstration were not at all satisfied. The recurrence of this issue on the agenda of recent summits shows the G7/G8 are sensitive to their criticism and cannot dismiss it. Their conscience is uneasy; they sense this is an issue that they have not got right yet. So this too will probably return to the G8 agenda.[12]

Institutional Consequences: The World Catches Up with the Summits

When the summits began, back in 1975, they had three distinctive features as an institution; dominance, rarity and bureaucratic independence. All three have been eroded over time.

Dominance

In the 1970s, the seven participating countries, plus the Commission and Presidency to represent the rest of the European Community, were the dominant powers in the international economic system. Whatever they could agree among themselves was likely to be accepted by others.

The G7/G8 members no longer dominate the world economically as they used to do. Many developing countries have become active players and influence international decisions. Some are very large and populous countries, like Brazil, China, India, Indonesia and Mexico. They are opening their big internal markets to foreign competition and are becoming internationally minded. Others are smaller economies that have grown rich from outward-looking policies and become trading powers and financial centres, like Hong Kong (China), Korea, Malaysia and Singapore. Despite the setback for some of these from the Asian financial crisis, the G8 has to pay more attention to their views and deal with them more tactfully and persuasively than in the past.

This dispersion of power in the world economic system is a consequence of globalisation. This has enabled developing countries to compete effectively with the mature economies of the West, to narrow the gap in living standards and become independent centres of power. This is the positive face of globalisation, to set against the worry that the poorest developing countries are falling further behind.

Rarity

In the 1970s the G7 was among the very few groups meeting regularly at head of government level. The only established cycle was the Commonwealth Heads of Government Meetings, held every two years. The European Council, also founded by Giscard, was just beginning. The North Atlantic Treaty Organisation (NATO) also met at summit level, but irregularly.

Since then, and especially in the last decade, international summit meetings have proliferated. NATO has a summit almost every year. The European Council not only has its regular cycle, twice a year, but holds special meetings as well, either on its own or with others. The UN has periodic summits on special issues: environment, population or social affairs. Regional and trans-regional bodies of more recent creation also meet at summit level: the Organisation of American States (OAS) for the Western hemisphere; Asia-Pacific Economic Co-operation (APEC) for the Asia-Pacific; the Organisation for Security and Cooperation in Europe (OSCE). Well-connected heads of state and government are always meeting their peers.

This proliferation of summits is both a tribute to the G7's pioneering role and another consequence of globalisation. As external factors intrude more deeply into domestic policy-making, heads of government no longer rely on sending their foreign secretaries or other specialist ministers to international meetings. They must take a hand themselves.

Bureaucratic Independence

The G7 summit began as a free-standing entity at head of government level. Other summits - Commonwealth, NATO, European Council - were each the apex of an established organisation. The G7 summit had its preparatory network formed of the personal representatives of the leaders, the "sher-pas". But the G7 did not exist at lower levels.

As the preceding point showed, other institutions, both global and regional, began by meeting at ministerial and official level and later completed their structures by adding a head of government layer. The G7 summit has now gone through this process in reverse.

For the first decade and more there was strong resistance from the leaders, especially the French Presidents Giscard and Mitterrand, to extending the G7 apparatus downwards. While US President Carter favoured a sort of summit bureaucracy, this was reversed when Reagan came to power. Specialist G7 groups were set up on occasion, but most had a limited life and were wound up once they had finished their work.

This resistance to bureaucracy started to erode seriously from the mid-1980s, with the emergence of G7 ministerial groups.[13] The earliest of these have established a degree of independence from the summits. This applies to the Quadrilateral or "Quad" composed of trade ministers from the US, EU, Japan and Canada. Its origins go back to Ottawa 1981. It acts as a pressure group in the WTO and its summit origins are forgotten. The G7 finance ministers emerged publicly at Tokyo 1986 and soon replaced the secretive G5, whose origins predate the summit itself. The G7 finance ministers meet as part of the summit framework; but they follow their own cycle for the rest of the year, always coming together on the margins of the IMF/IBRD spring and autumn meetings. Both trade and finance ministers have their apparatus of official deputies.

These groups have been followed by a network of G7/G8 meetings tied more closely to the summit cycle. Foreign ministers meet annually in September, on the margin of the UN General Assembly, to review the post-summit foreign policy agenda. Environment ministers meet every year a few weeks before the summit. Employment and finance ministers had by mid-1998 met three times to prepare for summits. Future meetings seem likely. Interior ministers had met twice on terrorism and crime. A distinct series of meetings, on various subjects, had been designed to embed the Russians in the G8 process; examples are the 1996 nuclear summit and the 1998 energy ministerial, both held in Moscow. There was a complete sequence of such specialist ministerial meetings in the six months before Birmingham.

Unlike the Quad and the G7 finance ministers, which fit neatly alongside the WTO and the IMF/IBRD, these newer groups may not correspond to an established global institution. All these ministerials also have their own supporting apparatus of officials. Alongside them, the preparation of the summit itself has generated another hierarchy of specialist groups of officials, on both economic and political subjects, preparing reports and papers for the sherpas or for the leaders themselves.

This expanding summit apparatus is not just the usual bureaucratic spread; the leaders could have kept that in check. The most powerful influence on this proliferation is the iterative way in which the summits work. The summits grapple with difficult and unfamiliar issues. They often need several attempts before hitting the right solution. They handle subjects for which there are no satisfactory global institutions. In these conditions, it becomes natural to create G7 or G8 groups to work on the issues between summits, to prepare future decisions and to keep track of problems, even when they have been handed on to wider institutions. These subsidiary groups, at ministerial or official level, gradually acquire a life of their own.

The G8 summit still has no headquarters, no written procedures and no secretariat. But in other respects it has become much less distinctive and much more like other institutions. The EU, NATO, APEC and the rest have completed their pyramids from the bottom upwards, finally adding an apex of heads of government. The G8 summit has grown its own pyramid from the top downwards, in a haphazard but all-embracing way. As a result, the summit apparatus has now reached the limit at which it can be managed by the host country for the summit in each year. The sherpas and their closest collaborators are caught between the demands of the leaders, for less paper and more time to talk among themselves; and the plethora of specialist advice and recommendations coming up from the host of other ministerial and official groups.

There are two possible ways to escape from this pressure. The first would be to create a separate summit secretariat. This has been advocated by outsiders almost since the summits began. But it has never had any appeal to the G8 governments and is not a serious proposition at the moment. The second solution is what is being adopted. It is to push more subjects downwards and outwards in the G8 hierarchy.

The consequence is that more G8 activity will become detached from the summit itself. The decisions of subordinate G8 groups will not have the authority of the summits themselves; but they will still carry weight because they are agreed by this influential group of countries. This already happens with the "Quad" of trade ministers and with the G7 finance ministers. Other G7 and G8 groups are likely to break their links with the summit and establish an independent existence. Some may start with the G7 or G8 members as their nucleus but add other countries.[14]

The decision to hold the 1998 summit among heads of government only, for the first time ever, should be seen in the light of this bureaucratic evolution. As long as the G7 summit was the source of decision-making on all subjects, foreign and finance ministers were not prepared to see the heads of government settling things on their own. This was felt most strongly in countries ruled by political coalitions, like Germany, Italy and Japan. It also applied in the United States, where - unlike other G7 countries - the President usually came to his high office without any previous ministerial experience. France, Britain and Canada had no such inhibitions about the leaders meeting on their own. But this group has been a minority in the G7; and previous attempts to promote a heads-only summit, notably by Canada before Halifax 1995, did not succeed.

But events moved on after Halifax. At the Lyon and Denver summits, though the heads and their ministers were all there, they held separate meetings. Plenary sessions, when heads and ministers gathered round the same table, were short and formal. It is thus less of a step to separate the meetings of the heads and their ministers in time as well as space. A similar decentralisation has happened to the preparatory process. Up to the early 1990s, sherpas usually met flanked by their foreign and finance ministry sous-sherpas. Now the sous-sherpas have their own networks of meetings and plenaries with all present are the exception.

So the first-ever heads-only summit, at Birmingham in 1998, does not mean the summit process is getting simpler. It is instead getting both more complex and more dispersed. The heads can meet on their own because established G7 or G8 machinery now exists for treating subjects at a lower level. It is thus easier to select a few issues which rise to the leaders themselves. This was not the intention of the summit's founders, Giscard and Schmidt. The process carries its own dangers: of G8 bureaucracy growing unchecked without the discipline of summit relevance; or of increased resistance from non-G8 countries to the spread of G8 groups unrelated to the summit. It is a natural reaction to the pressures of globalisation. But it makes the summit more like an ordinary institution.

Conclusion: Looking Beyond the Governments

This analysis is not intended to belittle the summits or their achievements;

far from it. It is intended to strip away some of the myths which surround this annual meeting of the world's' most influential economic leaders - myths which the leaders have sometimes encouraged themselves. It aims to show how the summits actually achieve their results.

The leaders make their contribution not by flashes of inspiration, but by sustained, iterative treatment of difficult issues. It often takes them several attempts to find acceptable solutions. Few problems can be settled definitively. They are prone to recur in a different form. In developing this iterative approach, the G8 summits have become less distinctive than they were. They are not single peaks, but part of the mountain range which makes up the international economic system.

The need for repeated treatment of problems has tended to clog up the summits' agenda. In the conditions of globalisation, when more and more international issues touch domestic policy and bid for the attention of heads of government, this congestion is inevitable. The escape is to extend the lower-level G8 apparatus, in a way which makes it easier for the leaders themselves to delegate. They could thus meet on their own for the first time at Birmingham in 1998, where they concentrated on the anxieties felt by their peoples about globalisation: loss of jobs; rising crime; the risks of financial panic; and the consequences of world poverty.

The response to globalisation has thus become a central focus for the summit. How should the leaders, now meeting on their own, best advance their objectives in the future? One approach would be to look beyond the activities of government. So far the G7/G8 summit has been a wholly governmental process. It involves national governments, the European Commission and inter-governmental bodies like the IMF, the WTO or the United Nations. But all this can now be left to their ministers, meeting separately. The heads can use their democratic legitimacy to look wider than government. They need to do so, both to reap the greatest benefits from globalisation and to overcome the resistance to it.

To maximise the benefits, the leaders need better links to the private business's community. To overcome the resistance to globalisation, they need to confront the network of pressure groups linked together on the Internet. These groups exploit the latest technology to mobilise campaigns which can frustrate government objectives. The G8 leaders should make the technology work for them and become consistent public advocates of the benefits of globalisation, to overcome their people's fears. Without such advocacy, the leaders may look down from the summit on a landscape clouded with doubt and uncertainty.

Notes

1   I began research into the summits, in collaboration with Professor Robert D Putnam, at the Royal Institute of International Affairs in 1982; Putnam and Bayne 1987 (first edition 1984) is the result. Later analyses are in Bayne 1992 and Bayne 1995, as well as in more recent pieces on the website of the University of Toronto G8 Research Group, http://www.g7.utoronto.ca. This paper draws heavily on this earlier work.

2   This theme is distinct from the study of summit compliance in the chapter of Ella Kokotsis and Joseph P. Daniels in this volume, though the two are related. This paper provides some reasons why summit compliance is less than optimal and explains what the summits try to do about it.

3   This view has been eloquently put by the late Dr Michael R. Hodges, in Hodges 1994 and his chapter in this volume.

4   The changing role of international organisations in the post-cold war world is examined in Reinalda and Verbeek 1998. The author's contribution to this book contains some comments on the place of the G7/G8 summit.

5   These issues were reviewed in the conference recorded at the Centre for Economic Performance in 1998, held at the London School of Economics and Political Science (LSE) ten days before the Birmingham summit. As Graham Ingham notes in the introduction: "We cannot claim that the conference provided an agenda which the G8 leaders followed. But it did provide an agenda for the longer term." See also Richard Layard's chapter in this volume.

6   This topic was treated by DeAnne Julius at the conference on 'Jobs, Crime and Money; Challenges for the G8 Summit in 1998' organised by Clifford Chance, the LSE and University of Toronto G8 Research Group in London on 13 May 1998. Her paper is published as Julius 1998.

7   The impact of globalisation on crime is analysed in Strange 1995 and the references given there. See also George Staple's chapter in this volume.

8   It is instructive to compare two papers on this subject from the Institute for International Economics. Bergsten and Henning 1996, writing at some distance from government, are very negative on the G7's performance. But Dobson 1991, drawing on her experience in the Canadian Department of Finance, finds some merit in the process of coordination as well as points requiring improvement.

9   The figure for total resources mobilised for the three countries is taken from Camdessus and Wolfensohn 1998. Since the Birmingham summit more has been found for Indonesia.

10 The British government broke this trend, by announcing in July 1998, a major increase in official aid funds over three years, taking it from 0.26% of GDP to 0.3% in 2001. See Financial Times, 15 July 1998, p. 11.

11 It is difficult to provide comparable figures for debt relief to the poorest. But the combined contribution of Paris Club, IMF and World Bank is estimated

as worth about $8 billion in the three years to 1998.

12   A fuller account of the summit's treatment of debt for the poorest is in Bayne 1998.

13   The impact of the G7/G8 apparatus as a system of world governance is well analysed in Kirton 1995 and his paper in this volume. Baker 1996, pp. 7-8, makes a fair point that Putnam and Bayne 1997 breaks off just as the G7 is starting to expand away from the summit.

14   A good recent example is the decision of the G8 foreign ministers, meeting specially on 12 June 1998 to discuss the Indian and Pakistani nuclear tests, to ask Argentina, Brazil, South Africa and Ukraine to join them, as countries which had renounced their capacity to make or deploy nuclear weapons. *Financial Times*, 13 June 1998, p. 3.

References

Baker, A. (1996), "The Historical Development of the G-7: An Incoherent and Disjointed Response to Global Interdependence?", G7RU Working Paper No. 2, School of Public Policy, Economics and Law, University of Ulster, Jordanstown, Northern Ireland.

Bayne, N. (1992), "The Course of Summitry", *The World Today*, vol. 48 no. 2, pp. 27-29.

Bayne, N. (1995), "The G7 Summit and the Reform of Global Institutions", *Government and Opposition*, vol. 30, no. 4, pp. 492-509.

Bayne, N. (1998), "Britain, the G8 and the Commonwealth: Lessons of the Birmingham Summit", *The Round Table*, no. 348.

Bergsten, C.F. and Henning, C.R. (1996), *Global Economic Leadership and the Group of Seven*, Institute for International Economics, Washington, D.C.

Camdessus, M. and Wolfensohn, J.D. (1998), "The Bretton Woods Institutions: Responding to the Asian Financial Crisis", in M. Fraser, ed., *The G8 and the World Economy*, Strategems Publishing Ltd., London, pp. 6-8.

Centre for Economic Performance (CEP) (1998), "Employability and Exclusion: What Governments Can Do", Papers from a Conference held on 6 May 1998 by the Centre for Economic Performance and the London School of Economics, London.

Dobson, W. (1991), "Economic Policy Coordination: Requiem or Prologue?", *Institute for International Economics*, Washington.

Hodges, M. (1994), "More Efficiency, Less Dignity: British Perspectives on the Future Role and Working of the G-7", *The International Spectator*, vol. XXIX, no. 2, pp. 141-159.

Julius, D. (1998), "Trade and Investment in the Light of the Asian Crisis", *Bank of England Quarterly Bulletin*, vol. 38 no. 3.

Kirton, J. (1995), "The Diplomacy of Concert: Canada, the G7 and the Halifax

Summit", *Canadian Foreign Policy*, vol. III, no.1, pp. 63-80.
Putnam, R.D. and Bayne, N. (1987), *Hanging Together: Cooperation and Conflict in the Seven-Power Summits*, SAGE, London.
Reinalda, B. and Verbeek, B. (eds) (1998), *Autonomous Policy Making by International Organizations*, Routledge, London and New York; especially, Bayne, N. "International Economic Organizations: More Policy Making, Less Autonomy", pp. 196-210.
Strange, S. (1995), "The Limits of Politics", *Government and Opposition*, vol. 30, no. 3, pp. 291-311.

3   Explaining G8 Effectiveness

JOHN J. KIRTON

FO2

Fa1 F41

Introduction

There are few international institutions as maligned, mistrusted and misunderstood as the Group of Seven (G7). To some, who focus only on the annual gathering of the leaders of the world's seven major market democracies and now Russia, the G7 is little more than a "global hot tub party". They feel it lacks the formal powers and organizational capacity of established international institutions such as the European Union (EU) or United Nations (UN) (Ikenberry, 1993; Smyser, 1993; Whyman, 1995).

To others, it is a closed club of an obsolescent rich white plutocracy, which lacks either legitimacy or effectiveness because it excludes such robust and rising powers as China, India, Indonesia and Brazil, and has yet to fully incorporate the new monetarily unified European Union (Commission on Global Governance, 1995; ul Haq, 1994; Jayarwedna, 1989; Labbohm, 1995; De Silguy, 1997; Henning, 1996).

To still others, it is a club that has not lived up to its potential in the 1990's, due to a false new consensus that its leaders lack the power to perform its core functions of macroeconomic management in a world where markets and multinationals dominate (Bergsten and Henning, 1996). Gone is the recent optimism that heralded the G7 as a governing global concert at the dawn of the post-cold war decade (Lewis, 1991-2; Odum, 1995). There are few who proclaim its centrality, effectiveness or even potential now (Bayne, 1995; Ionescu, 1995; Kirton and Kokotsis, 1998).

The prevailing pessimism, however, stands in sharp contrast to the observed proliferation and performance of the G7 over the past decade. From 1989 onward Russia has been admitted, ultimately as a full member, many other countries have become associated through a variety of innovative mechanisms, and several contenders, for reasons of status and function, continue to quietly press their case for inclusion. The G7's agenda has expanded as the linked economic and political issues that inspired its creation have been joined by a host of subjects once considered entirely domestic but which now clearly call for a coordinated transnational response on a global basis.

With the broadened agenda has come deeper institutionalization, domestic engagement and participation by civil society actors. Indeed, the annual gathering of the leaders is now supplemented by a year-round sequence of ad hoc meetings of the leaders and their finance and foreign ministers, regular forums collectively embracing a majority of the ministries of government, and a subterranean web of working groups that even the leaders' personal representatives find it difficult to monitor and control.

Finally, despite periodic delays and disappointments, the G7 of the past decade has produced substantial achievements in international co-operation, constraining its members' behaviour in accordance with its collective commitments, and responding to the major crises of the moment. In short, as the post cold war, globalizing world of the 1990s moves into the new millennium, the G7 and now Group of Eight (G8) is emerging as an effective centre, and is prospectively the effective centre, of global governance.

Created to contain the offensive of a communist east and largely socialist south in the 1970s, combating an expansionist USSR in the new cold war of the 1980s, and emerging victorious in the 1990's, the G7 and its core values of a market economy and democratic polity have now acquired a global predominance. But its enduring and enlarging success in forwarding, against formidable resistance, the new core values of inclusive democracy, ecologically sustainable market economies, and international openness and engagement rests on several deeper foundations. The first is a growing systemic predominance of capability from, and equality of capability among, G7 and now G8 members, as Russia's inclusion has removed the major outside rival, and as the hard military capabilities where the United States predominated have diminished in relevance in the new era. The second, amidst rampant regionalism, is a growing interdependence among G7 members, whose increasingly deep integration and international exposure is generating a common intervulnerability that forces them to co-operate (Nye and Keohane, 1977; Doran, 1985).

Providing a shared trust, epistemology and reference point for co-operative solutions, despite the inevitable systems friction, is the common commitment to core democratic market values, and the edifice of more specific principles such as human rights and social equity constructed on them. Finally, the increasing capacity of the G7 system to provide political control by popularly and democratically elected leaders has enabled it to make the high-level linkages and provide the detailed oversight of once domestic issues that governance in the new era of the coming millennium requires.

The G7's Growth as a New Millennium Institution

The most visible sign of the G8's emergence as the centre of global governance for the new millennium is its recent institutional development. This development is evident in the dimensions of membership, agenda, ministerial and official level involvement, domestic engagement and civil society participation. Increasingly, the G7 is coming to resemble the inner cabinet of the global polity, compactly including all globally-oriented countries, embracing the full public policy agenda, and engaging the multilateral international bureaucracies, and most departments of national government at the ministerial and official level. It is thus uniquely tailored to deal with the intensifying linkages across the global agenda and between processes at the international and domestic levels.

Membership

The first dimension of institutional growth is the G7's expanding membership and participation. As Table 3.1 reveals, there is a clear logic to the G7's membership, which has been manifest virtually without exception during

Table 3.1	Participation in the G7 Summit, 1975 - (by country or international organization involved)
1976	Canada
1977	European Union (President of the Commission)
1982	Belgium as President of the Council of the EU (also in 1987)
1986	Netherlands as President of the EU (also in 1991, 1997)
1989	G15-G7 Pre-Summit Dinner
1991	USSR-G7 Post Summit Meeting
1992	Russia-G7 Post Summit Meeting (1994 P8, 1996 Moscow, 1997, 1998)
1993	Indonesia's Pre-Summit Dinner with Host Japan and US
1996	Ukraine (as Moscow Nuclear Safety Summit)
1996	IMF, IBRD, WTO, UN Session and Lunch with G7

Note: excludes non-immediate, off-site pre and post Summit consultation by host or individual G7 member, even when operating with a G7 mandate.

Source: Compiled by John Kirton, University of Toronto

the institution's first twenty-four years. As a classic concert it includes only, and all of, the world's major powers (Kirton, 1993, 1989). As a modern concert those major powers must have durable market economies and democratic polities, despite the diversity of the particular forms they display. Finally, G7 membership and market democracy are forever. That is, the G7 will maintain the inclusion and power of embattled members, such as Italy in 1976 and Russia in 1998, but will also act collectively to ensure that they do not depart from their market-oriented democratic core. Today's often-touted prospective entrants - China, India, Indonesia, Brazil - will only be admitted if and when, in the still distant future, they become enduring market-oriented, democratic major powers, and thus acquire the fully systemic perspective, sense of responsibility and capacity to contribute to global order which flows from these attributes.

Such coherence at the core has allowed for creative ways of associating outsiders, and thus enhancing the legitimacy and effectiveness of G7 governance. While the Netherlands, Belgium and Australia were denied admission in their own right in the initial years, the former two were represented, along with other European democratic, market-oriented middlepowers, through the head of the European Commission/Union in 1977 and subsequently through their Prime Ministers when their Presidency of the Commission/Union and the annual summit coincided.

The year 1989 inaugurated a process of summit dialogue with leaders of major developing countries, first when the new Group of 15 (G15) dined with the G7 on the eve of the opening of the Paris "Summit of the Arch" and subsequently in 1993 when the leaders of host Japan and the US met on the eve of the summit with Indonesia's Suharto, then head of the still-functioning "Non-Aligned" Movement. The ad hoc 1996 Moscow nuclear safety summit (and 1994 Winnipeg Ministerial) brought Ukraine in for the moment. Lyon in 1996 saw a post-summit G7 lunch with the leaders of the world's four major multilateral organizations. The 1998 London finance ministerial repeated the formula for the International Monetary Fund (IMF), the International Bank for Reconstruction and Development (IBRD), and the World Trade Organisation (WTO). Michael Camdessus's May 1998 concept of a meeting every two years of the G7 with the IMF's Group of 24 (G24) presents a promising proposal for expanded participation in the future. In addition there are a host of pre- and post-summit consultations with wider constituencies and many G7 created bodies - covering subjects from missile technology control to the global information society - that have quickly expanded to include a wider group.

Future alterations in the current membership are likely to be slow and incremental. Although Birmingham brought the birth of the full G8, it also marked a continuation and strengthening of the existing G7, whose leaders met, when they were fresh, immediately before the G8 officially opened, for a serious treatment of the new international financial architecture, the Japanese and G7 economies, Ukraine, and Russia itself. Some now see the inclusion of Russia and the advent of European Monetary Union (EMU) as leading to a new Group of Three (G3) (Henning, 1996). However, the residual relevance of Britain and Canada, the operation of the 16 year old trade ministers Quadrilateral, and the need to mobilize continental European leaders and finance ministers to contain any new financial crisis of Asian dimensions casts severe doubt on this easy conclusion.

The economic collapse of Indonesia, concerns about China on several dimensions and the difficulties faced by the UN Security Council about which and how many new members to include provide strong support for the status quo. At the same time, one can look to more regular dialogues with multilateral organizations and new ways to include important constituencies, such as central and eastern Europe through the EU, and the Asia-Pacific Economic Co-operation (APEC) forum through the G7's four Pacific members.

Agenda

With expanding participation has come a proliferating G7 agenda. The G7 began with a focus on both economic and political issues and the relationship between the two, as the 1970s challenge of "stagflation" and the ensuing "crisis of governability" required an integrated, high level response. The summit soon added transnational security threats such as terrorist aircraft hijacking and regional security threats from ever more distant reaches of the globe. As Table 3.2 indicates, the 1990s brought a much expanded array of transnational issues - with the global environment, infectious disease and international crime added.

At the same time, as Table 3.3 demonstrates, topics once considered entirely domestic - employment, pension plans, education, social security nets, welfare reform - have arisen to occupy centre stage. With this trend, and the decision of the British hosts to make employment and crime two of the three core subjects at Birmingham in 1998 - the G7 has become an important global centre for domestic governance.

Table 3.2   The G7 Agenda, 1989-96

Issues	1989	1990	1991	1992	1993	1994	1995	1996
Macroeconomic	14	11	-	13	7	-	-	12
Microeconomic	3	2	-	-	-	6	9	4
Trade	7	12	8	-	2	-	-	11
Development	13	14	12	-	3	-	-	12
IFI Reform	-	2	-	-	-	-	-	10
Environment	32	-	11	2	2	6	-	-
Drugs	2	6	6	-	-	-	-	-
Aids	1	-	-	-	-	-	-	-
Central/East Europe	-	15	12	18	3	11	-	5
Energy	-	-	5	-	-	-	-	-
Nuclear Safety	-	-	-	8	-	7	-	-
Trans-national Organized Crime	-	-	-	-	-	4	-	-
Middle East	-	-	2	-	-	-	-	-
Migration	-	-	1	-	-	-	-	-
UN Reform	-	-	-	-	-	3	-	-

Table 3.3   The G7's Microeconomic Agenda, 1988-96
             (Most Common Issues in Economic Declarations)

1.	Education/Vocational Training	8
2.	Unemployment Reduction	7
3.	Technological Innovation	6
4.	Regulatory Reform	5
5.	Tax Reform	4
6.	Social System Reform	4
7.	Enhanced Competition Strengthening	4
8.	Saving and Investment Encouragement	4
9.	Labour Market Flexibility	3
10.	Social Security Flexibility	3
11.	Global Information Society	2

Source: Compiled by John Kirton, University of Toronto

Institutional Depth

A proliferating G7 agenda has brought a deepening of G7 institutions. As Table 3.4 shows, at the ministerial level the three stand-alone G7 forums born in the 1980s - for trade in 1982, foreign affairs in 1984 and finance in 1986 - all dealt with traditional international issues. Those of the 1990s - the environment in 1992, employment in 1994, information in 1995 and terrorism in 1995 - all addressed more classically domestic matters. The years 1997-8 have added ministerial meetings for small and medium enterprise (SME), crime and energy. To support these and other G7 networks there has emerged dozens of official level working groups that often operate beyond the detailed knowledge or control of the G7 sherpas.

Table 3.4   The G7 System of Institutions

Leaders:
  Annual G7 Summit, 1975-
  Ad Hoc Summits, 1985 (New York), 1996 (Moscow)

On-Site Ministerial Forums:
  Annual Finance Ministers Summit-Site Meetings, 1975-
  Annual Foreign Ministers Summit Site Meetings, 1975-
  Trade Ministers Meetings, 1978, 1993, 1995

Stand-Alone Ministerial Forums:
  Trade Ministers Quadrilateral, 1982-
  Foreign Ministers, 1984-
  Finance Ministers, 1986-
  Environment, 1992, 1994-
  Employment, March 1994 (Detroit), April 1996 (Lille), January 1998 (Britain)
  Information, February 1995 (Brussels), May 1996 (Midrand)[a]
  Terrorism, December 1995 (Ottawa), July 1996 (Paris)

Ad Hoc Ministerial Meetings:
  Russian Financial Assistance, April 1993, Tokyo
  Ukraine Financial Assistance, October 1994, Winnipeg
  Small and Medium Enterprise, Spring 1997, Bonn
  Crime, December 1997, Washington
  Energy Ministers, Spring 1998, Russia

[a]More than G7 members present

Source: Compiled by John Kirton, University of Toronto

Taken together, as Table 3.5 shows, G7 co-operation now engages a clear majority of the important departments of member governments, giving the G7 system a degree of domestic engagement it never previously exercised. With the direct involvement of major corporations in the Global Information Society (GIS) and energy ministerials, and other non-governmental organisations in the SME and environment ministerials, domestic engagement is starting to extend to the participation of civil society actors. This direct domestic relevance and nascent democratization of the G7 is the foundation for the institution in the new millennium.

Table 3.5	Ministers Involved in G7 Forums, 1975-
	(by date of first participation by an individual member)
1975	Foreign Affairs (State)
1975	Finance (Treasury, Exchequer)
1978	Economics (Germany)
1982	Trade (Japan, Quadrilateral)
1989	Environment (US, 1992- Ministerial)
1990	Agriculture (US at Houston)
1994	Human Resources (Canada), Employment
1994	Labour
1995	Industry (GIS)
1995	Heritage (GIS)
1995	Solicitor General, Interior (Terrorism)
1995	Transportation (US for Land Transportation Security)
1995	Justice
1997	Small and Medium Sized Enterprises
1998	Energy

Source: Compiled by John Kirton, University of Toronto

This institutional dynamism shows few signs of being contained. There are important concerns about the paralyzing "bureaucratization" of the summit as a development which contradicts the forum's seminal purpose and precious feature of political control by democratically and popularly elected heads of state and government. Birmingham responded to this concern by producing the never before realized ideal of Rambouillet - having leaders meet alone without attending finance and foreign ministers. However, those ministers met alone and jointly in London the previous weekend, both to deal with their own lengthy agenda and to prepare the core items the leaders discussed the following weekend.

The initial experience with the new format has led the G8 leaders to repeat it for Köln in 1999 (with the ministers slated to meet several weeks earlier). It also inspired the G7 foreign ministers to look with some favour on going beyond their one meeting a year (in September) to a more frequent (probably twice a year) schedule. The innovative format of Birmingham has thus significantly expanded the institutional capacity of the G7, creating, at least for the officials attending both weekend gatherings, a responsibility to maintain coherence over a full ten days of G7 summitry in 1998.

Institutionalization, however, does not presage a formal international organization. Although not all G7 ministers are popularly elected, the expansion of the ministerial system has reinforced the key G7 feature of political control. The G7's one small foray into creating an organization of its own - the Support Implementation Group (SIG) in Moscow - has now ended. And despite occasional pleas by outsiders, there is no desire to create a G7 Secretariat. Future energies will concentrate on rejuvenating and modernizing existing multilateral organizations, improving the coherence and political control of the maze of G7 working groups, and developing networks, perhaps at times involving civil society actors, to perform tasks conducted by intergovernmental organizations in an earlier age. Such a model makes the G7 well adapted to a world in which the single authority centres of old are being supplemented by others in a more multi-centred, interactive world (Deibert, 1997).

The G8's Growing Co-operation, Compliance and Crisis Management

A further sign of the G7's emergence as an effective centre of global governance is the improving and relatively high performance it has achieved during the 1990s in its core functions of forging co-operative agreements, inducing national compliance with those collective commitments, and responding to regional crises before they endanger systemic stability.

During its first two cycles, the ability of the G7 summit to generate ambitious, timely and well-tailored agreements varied widely from year to year, as scored by the classic evaluation of the summit's performance during those years (Putnam and Bayne, 1987). However, as Table 3.6 displays, amidst this high volatility, there was a three stage sequence, consisting of high performance from 1975 to 1979, low performance from 1980 to 1984 and medium performance in 1986 and 1987 (Kirton, 1989). The pattern of the most recent decade, based on a modified application of the Putnam-Bayne scoring system, suggests a return to relatively high levels of performance. What is particularly striking is the consistency in this performance, with only the 1994 Naples summit and especially the 1997 Denver summit being poor performance outliers. This consistency may reflect the deepening institutionalization of the summit system in the 1990s, providing a firmer foundation of preparation and progress than the unreinforced leaders-sherpa process of earlier times.

This consistency is appropriate to the sustained impetus the G7 has given to central processes of system transformation during the 1990's, in contrast to the sole, often crisis-response achievements of the apparently permanent cold war system of earlier decades. The central contemporary achievement has been the largely peaceful end of the cold war and Soviet Union, and the transformation of the remnant Russia into a stable, market-oriented, democratic polity, as the G7 incrementally and judiciously pro-

Table 3.6   Co-operative Achievements of G7 Summits, 1988-97
(Putnam and Bayne scoring model)

1975	Rambouillet	A-	Monetary reform
1976	Puerto Rico	D	Nothing Significant
1977	London I	B-	Trade; growth; nuclear power
1978	Bonn I	A	Growth, energy and trade
1979	Tokyo I	B+	Energy
1980	Venice	C+	Afghanistan; energy
1981	Ottawa	D	Nothing significant
1982	Versailles	C	East-West trade; surveillance
1983	Williamsburg	B	Euromissiles
1984	London II	C-	Debt
1985	Bonn II	E	Nothing significant
1986	Tokyo II	B-	Terrorism; surveillance
1987	Venice II	D	Nothing significant
1988	Toronto	B	
1989	Paris	A-	
1990	Houston	B	
1991	London 3	B+	
1992	Munich	B-	
1993	Tokyo 3	A-	Trade
1994	Naples	B-	
1995	Halifax	A-	
1996	Lyon	B+	
1997	Denver	C-	
1998	Birmingham	A-	

Note: 1975 to 1986 scores come from Putnam and Bayne (1987), pp.270. The scores since 1987 were assigned by reviewing all published writings on the G7 by Putnam and Bayne individually or jointly, identifying their judgments on the individual Summits as Putnam and Bayne compared each to others since and before 1987, and assigning grades that reflected these ordinal rankings and the degree of the variation. The calculations were made by Ella Kokotsis. These scores from 1988 onward were then reviewed confirmed and adjusted by Sir Nicholas Bayne. Such a system provides robust guarantees against systemic biases in both the overall level of and range of variation within this contemporary set.

vided large-scale financial assistance, and participation in the G7 itself to reinforce domestic coalitions that conduced to this end (Kirton, 1999). This process, begun with the Gorbachev letter at Paris 1989, was completed at Birmingham with the transformation of the G7 into a G8. A second achievement has come, in the realm of north-south relations, in relieving the debt of the poorest, a process begun at Toronto in 1988 and advanced to within reach of completion at Birmingham in 1998. Another has been in global environmental protection, where G7 leadership provided important assistance in concluding the Rio conventions and subsequent additions dealing with high seas overfishing. Further pointing to a record of routine high accomplishment is the large number of concrete commitments for sustainable development and assistance to Russia the G7 has generated from 1988 to 1995 (Kokotsis, 1999; Kokotsis and Kirton, 1997).

The summits of the 1990s have also been effective in constraining the actions of their members, as judged by the record of the latter in complying with the major concrete commitments they collectively encode in the summit communiqué. Although direct overtime comparisons are difficult to make due to the different methodologies employed, and while compliant behaviour may result from factors other than summit commitments, the overall pattern is suggestive. Von Furstenberg and Daniels, examining compliance with G7 economic and energy commitments from 1975 to 1989, found a weak but positive performance of 30.7%, with Britain and Canada complying the most, and compliance highest in the areas of international trade and energy (Von Furstenberg and Daniels, 1992; Daniels, 1993). Kokostis' exploration of United States and Canadian compliance with G7 sustainable development commitments from 1988 to 1995 shows a slight increase in overall compliance levels, with particularly high levels for Canada, a sharp rise in US compliance from the previous era, and very high levels of compliance in the area of assistance to Russia (Kokotsis and Kirton, 1997; Kokotsis, 1999).

An analysis of compliance of commitments in 19 issues areas at the 1996 Lyon summit by the G7 Research Group shows an overall level of 30.7% for economic issues, 47.5% for transnational issues, and 31% for security issues, with the highest compliance coming from Germany, Canada, the United States and Britain (G7 Research Group, 1998a). A similar analysis of compliance with the 1997 Denver commitments in six key areas (crime, development, employment, environment, landmines, and Russia) reveals an overall compliance record of 57.6%, led by Britain and Japan, and the areas of landmines and the environment (G7 Research Group, 1998b).

The summits of the 1990s have also acquired a respectable record in responding to, if not anticipating and preventing, regional crises which threaten the stability of the global system. In the defining case of the Asian financial crisis of 1997-8, collective G7 action was more robust, came at an earlier stage and has been far more effective through to the spring of 1998 than the US-centric effort in the Mexican peso crisis of 1994 (Kirton and Kokotsis, 1998; Kirton, 1995a; Kirton, 1995b). In addition to the far reaching agreements forged by the G7 finance ministers at Hong Kong in September 1997 to reform the international financial system, by November the G7 was acting collectively to create a second line of defence to reinforce IMF reserves. By December it had activated its second line to successfully stem the assault by markets on Korea, and subsequently acted to punitively single out an Indonesia still unwilling to reform. Meetings of G8 finance deputies in the summer of 1998 also helped Japan implement the measures agreed to at Birmingham, notably providing adequate fiscal stimulus to revive the domestic and Asian economy, and acting to clear up its bad bank debts.

Causes of G8 Effectiveness

The causes of the G7's growing effectiveness as a centre of global governance lie in the four foundations identified by a modified concert equality model of G7 performance - equalizing capabilities, intensifying interdependence activated by crisis, common principles and problems, and multi-level political control.

Equalizing Capabilities

The concert equality model predicts, firstly, that summit success emerges when America is rendered multilaterally-inclined and modest by the superior economic performance of its G7 partners rather than standing egocentrically triumphant by its superior capabilities, growth and performance. Thus, as Table 3.7 shows, the high summit success of the 1970s came as American growth was exceeded by that of commodity-rich Canada, Japan and Italy and equaled by that of France. The poor performance of the early 1980s came as the US moved toward its Reagan revival ascendancy from 1983 to 1985. But summit success returned with the more modest America of 1986-1991. The return of American primacy in 1992 and 1993 may help explain the failure of Naples, while the equality of Halifax in 1995 underlay the achievements of that year.

A similar portrait emerges more sharply by examining America's share of G7 capabilities measured by Gross National Product (GNP) at current exchange rates each year. As Table 3.8 and Figure 3.1 indicate, the US share fell from 45.5% to 41.1% from 1975 to 1980, jumped to 51.7% by 1985, and then fell steadily from that peak to 38.2% in 1995. Since then

Table 3.7		**Real GDP** (Percentage changes from previous period)						
	US	**Japan**	**Germany**	**France**	**Italy**	**UK**	**Canada**	**EU**
1970-79[a]	3.5	4.6	2.9	3.5	3.6	2.4	4.9	3.2
1980	0.3	2.8	1.0	1.6	3.5	(2.2)	1.5	1.4
1981	2.5	3.2	0.1	1.2	0.5	(1.3)	3.7	0.1
1982	2.1	3.1	(0.9)	2.5	0.5	1.7	(3.2)	0.9
1983	4.0	2.3	1.8	0.7	1.2	3.7	3.2	1.7
1984	6.8	3.9	2.8	1.3	2.6	2.3	6.3	2.3
1985	3.7	4.4	2.0	1.9	2.8	3.8	4.8	2.6
1986	3.0	2.9	2.3	2.5	2.8	4.3	3.3	2.8
1987	2.9	4.2	1.5	2.3	3.1	4.8	4.2	2.9
1988	3.8	6.2	3.7	4.5	3.9	5.0	5.0	4.2
1989	3.4	4.8	3.6	4.3	2.9	2.2	2.4	3.5
1990	1.3	5.1	5.7	2.5	2.2	0.4	(0.2)	3.0
1991	1.0	4.0	5.0	0.8	1.1	(2.0)	(1.8)	1.5
1992	2.7	1.1	2.2	1.2	0.6	(0.5)	0.8	0.9
1993	2.3	0.1	(1.1)	(1.3)	(1.2)	2.1	2.2	(0.5)
1994	3.5	0.5	2.9	2.8	2.1	3.8	4.1	2.9
1995	2.0	0.9	1.9	2.2	3.0	2.4	2.3	2.5
1996[b]	2.4	3.6	1.1	1.3	0.8	2.4	1.5	1.6
1997[b]	2.2	1.6	2.2	2.5	1.2	3.3	3.3	2.4
1998[b]	2.0	3.7	2.6	2.6	2.1	3.0	3.3	2.7

[a] Average of the ten years
[b] Estimates and Projections

Source: OECD Economic Outlook

the US has experienced a second if much milder "Clinton" restoration, increasing to 42.1% by 1997. This recent rise set the stage for the damaging triumphalism President Clinton displayed at Denver that year.

The importance of equal and equalizing capabilities is further evident through an examination of the specialized capabilities most relevant to the continuous core areas of the summit agenda. While America has always led in absolute GNP and by a wide margin in virtually all financial indicators, it has not done so in either of the other two - trade and official development assistance (ODA). In trade, Germany has had an occasional lead. By 1997,

Table 3.8   Relative Capability of Major Powers in the International System, 1950-96 (Ratio U.S. GNP in current U.S.$ exchange rates)

Year	US	Japan	Germany	France	Italy	UK	Canada	Russia	China	US%G-9	US%G-8	US%G-7
1950	100	3.8	7.3	9.0	4.5	15.3	5.4	5.6	NA	NA	NA	68.6
1955	100	5.5	NA	NA	NA	NA	6.4	7.1	9.6	59.4	NA	65.9
1960	100	7.6	16.5	14.2	8.5	14.7	6.5	8.7	NA	NA	NA	62.0
1965	100	12.2	16.9	13.5	9.4	12.3	7.9	34.2	6.8	46.4	NA	57.4
1970	100	19.8	18.8	14.5	9.3	12.1	8.3	32.2	9.1	44.6	52.0	54.6
1974	100	32.3	27.3	18.8	10.8	13.6	10.3	32.5	9.9	39.1	44.8	46.9
1975	100	32.9	27.5	22.2	11.5	14.9	10.7	32.9	10.2	38.0	43.4	45.5
1976	100	33.3	26.3	20.1	11.1	13.1	11.5	30.1	8.6	39.3	44.6	46.4
1977	100	36.7	27.4	20.2	11.4	13.2	10.5	29.0	8.8	38.9	43.8	45.6
1978	100	46.1	30.4	22.4	12.4	14.9	9.7	29.5	10.1	36.3	40.6	42.4
1979	100	41.9	31.9	24.1	13.6	17.1	9.6	28.2	10.8	36.1	40.2	42.0
1980	100	40.0	31.3	25.1	15.2	20.1	9.8	27.4	11.5	35.4	39.3	41.1
1981	100	39.3	23.5	19.6	12.0	17.1	9.8	23.2	9.6	39.3	43.3	45.2
1982	100	35.5	21.6	17.8	11.4	15.8	9.8	23.6	9.0	40.9	45.3	47.2
1983	100	36.0	20.0	15.8	10.8	13.9	9.9	22.5	8.9	42.0	46.4	48.4
1984	100	33.7	16.6	13.4	11.0	11.4	9.2	18.8	8.0	45.0	49.2	51.2
1985	100	33.5	15.7	13.2	10.6	11.4	8.8	17.5	7.3	45.9	49.9	51.7
1986	100	46.7	21.2	17.4	14.3	13.6	8.6	19.9	6.7	40.2	43.8	45.1
1987	100	53.0	24.9	19.7	16.9	15.2	9.2	21.2	6.8	37.5	40.7	41.8
1988	100	60.3	25.0	19.9	17.3	17.3	10.1	21.6	7.9	35.8	38.9	40.0
1989	100	55.9	23.2	18.7	16.9	16.3	10.6	20.9	6.6	37.2	40.3	41.4
1990	100	53.4	27.3	21.8	19.9	17.8	10.4	NA	6.2	NA	38.9	39.9
1991	100	59.2	28.1	21.1	20.4	17.8	10.3	13.8	6.6	36.1	37.9	38.9
1992	100	61.5	30.0	22.2	20.5	17.5	9.5	5.3	7.0	36.6	37.3	38.3
1993	100	67.1	27.2	19.9	15.8	14.4	8.7	1.7	8.5	38.0	38.2	39.5
1994	100	68.4	26.1	18.9	14.9	14.4	7.9	1.3	8.9	36.0	36.1	39.9
1995	100	64.6	33.2	21.5	15.4	15.0	7.8	NA	NA	NA	NA	38.2
1996	100	56.5	29.8	19.7	16.0	16.5	7.6	NA	NA	NA	NA	40.6
1997b	100	54.0	27.1	17.8	14.7	16.3	7.7	NA	NA	NA	NA	42.1

a Russia refers to the USSR prior to 1990

b Data for 1997 is preliminary and corresponds to OECD, Main Economic Indicators. It has been calculated at current prices and exchange rates.

Source: IMF International Financial Statistics, OECD Main Economic Indicators, UN National Accounts Statistics, The Economist

Figure 3.1   Inequality of Capability among G7 Powers, 1950-97

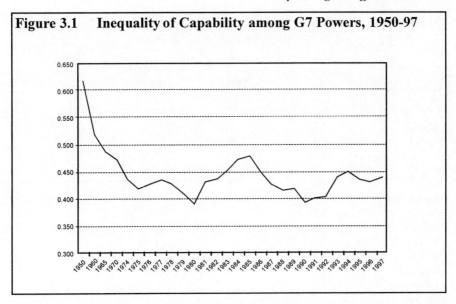

as Table 3.9 shows, even with the US again in first, there was substantial equality across the seven (who collectively, without exception, led the world). It is in trade that the G7 has been highly successful, both in reaching co-operative agreements and above all in securing national compliance. In development, as Table 3.10 shows, equality is even more pronounced, as America's loss of primacy in the 1990 s has set the stage for the G7's achievements in this area over the past decade. Similarly, successful summit co-operation and compliance over the past decade in assistance to the former Soviet Union and the environment (as with energy before), can be explained by the relative expenditures deployed, respectively, by Germany (on a per capita basis) and Canada in these spheres. Thus, even at moments of overall US primacy, as at Denver in 1997, co-operative success tends to come in those areas - Africa, the environment, Russian participation - where America is most equal.

This issue structure model not only explains the pattern of summit performance by individual issue area. It also provides a foundation for over-all equality in a forum where the agenda is comprehensive and issues are often inherently, epistemically, or tactically linked. Carefully constructed tactical linkage can lead to the great package deals as featured at Bonn in 1978. Other forms of linkage lead, more routinely, to member countries mobilizing different capabilities - market access, debt relief, financial assistance - to accomplish a shared objective.

Table 3.9	Merchandise Exports and Trade Openness, 1997

(US$ billion, as percentage of world total)

Country	Export	X as% GDP 1997	X as% GDP 1992
USA	12.6	11.8%	10.2%
Germany	9.4	26.6%	23.7%
Japan	7.7	11.1%	10.1%
France	5.3	31.4%	27.1%
Britain	5.1	28.4%	23.8%
Italy	4.4	24.4%	17.8%
Canada	3.9	40.2%	27.2%
Netherlands	3.5		
Hong Kong	3.4		
China	3.3		
Belgium/L	3.1		
S. Korea	2.5		
Singapore	2.3		
Taiwan	2.2		
Mexico	2.0		
Spain	1.9		
Russia	1.6		

Notes:

G7 Total = 48.4

G8 Total = 50.0 (with Russia)

G9 Total = 58.5 (with EU's Netherlands, Belgium & Luxembourg, Spain)

The volume of U.S. exports in 1997 was U.S. $689 billion.

Source: The Economist, March 28, 1998, p. 101, using WTO data; Canada, Birmingham G8 summit and Official Visits in Europe by Prime Minister Jean Chretien, May 13-12, 1998, Background Information

Interdependence Activated by Crisis

These structural factors provide a powerful if crude underlying cause of high summit performance. Activating this heterogeneous constellation of equalized capabilities is the high, broadening and equalizing interdependence and resulting intervulnerability among G7 members, at times rendered acute by crises within or without. Such interdependence is taking place on a global rather than regional basis, reinforcing the centrality of the G7. To be sure, the major moves in European monetary integration, APEC, the North American Free Trade Area (NAFTA) and the Free Trade Area of the Americas (FTAA) have provided a powerful thrust toward the regionaliza-

Table 3.10 Official Aid Expenditures, 1993, 1997
(Countries spending over 1 USB, billion US$)

Country	1993	1997
Japan	11.3	9.4
USA	9.0	6.1
France	7.9	6.2
Germany (West)	6.8	6.0
Britain	2.9	3.8
Italy	2.9	1.9
Holland	2.5	3.6
Canada	2.1	2.8
Sweden	1.7	2.4
Denmark	1.3	2.4
Spain	1.3	1.9
Norway	1.0	2.0
Australia	1.0	1.8

Source: OECD as printed in The Economist, July 9, 1994, p. 106, June 27, 1998, p. 107

tion of the world economy (Kirton, 1997a; Kirton, 1997b; Weintraub, 1997). However the members of the G7 exhibit high interdependence by remaining heavily dependent on trade relations with one another, even as their inter-vulnerability increases as their economies generally become more open to international trade.

As Table 3.11 indicates, from 1975 to 1990 G7 members trade with one another increased from about 50% to 75%. Despite a small decline since, especially for the EU, intra-G7 trade has remained at levels much higher than those of 1975. As Table 3.9 shows, all G7 economies have become more internationally open and trade dependent over the past half decade, a component of G7-driven policy globalization which is transforming this transregional interdependence into intervulnerability. Such trends are highly likely to continue. In the case of the US, the share of Gross Domestic Product (GDP) accounted for by trade rose from 10% in 1970 to 15% in 1980, 23% by 1996 and a projected 34% as the new millennium opens (USTR, 1997). Reflecting the leadership by G7 members other than the US in some financial domains, and thus displaying the effective equality in burden sharing on a transregional basis to prevent systemic crises (Kindleberger, 1973), were the contributions in the Asian financial crisis second line of defense. Japan gave US$ 10 billion, the US provided $5 billion, the four European G7 members contributed $1.25 billion each and Canada up to $1 billion.

Table 3.11   Intra-G7 Exports, 1975, 1990, 1995
(as percentage of total exports)

1975

From/To	US	Japan	Germany	UK	France	Canada	Italy	EEC	Total
US	0.00	0.09	0.05	0.04	0.03	0.20	0.03	0.07	0.50
Japan	0.20	0.00	0.03	0.03	0.01	0.02	0.01	0.03	0.32
Germany	0.06	0.01	0.00	0.05	0.12	0.01	0.07	0.20	0.51
UK	0.09	0.02	0.06	0.00	0.06	0.03	0.03	0.17	0.45
France	0.04	0.01	0.16	0.06	0.00	0.01	0.09	0.16	0.54
Canada	0.62	0.06	0.02	0.05	0.01	0.00	0.01	0.03	0.80
Italy	0.07	0.01	0.19	0.05	0.13	0.01	0.00	0.09	0.53
EEC	0.18	0.06	0.34	0.08	0.13	0.02	0.05	0.00	0.86

1990

From/To	US	Japan	Germany	UK	France	Canada	Italy	EEC	Total
US	0.00	0.12	0.05	0.06	0.03	0.21	0.02	0.10	0.60
Japan	0.32	0.00	0.06	0.04	0.02	0.02	0.01	0.07	0.54
Germany	0.07	0.03	0.00	0.08	0.13	0.01	0.09	0.32	0.73
UK	0.13	0.03	0.13	0.00	0.11	0.02	0.07	0.27	0.74
France	0.06	0.02	0.17	0.09	0.00	0.01	0.11	0.26	0.72
Canada	0.75	0.06	0.02	0.02	0.01	0.00	0.01	0.03	0.89
Italy	0.08	0.02	0.19	0.07	0.16	0.01	0.00	0.20	0.74
EEC	0.05	0.07	0.33	0.08	0.08	0.00	0.07	0.00	0.67

1995

From/To	US	Japan	Germany	UK	France	Canada	Italy	EEC	Total
US	0.00	0.11	0.04	0.05	0.02	0.22	0.02	0.08	0.54
Japan	0.28	0.00	0.05	0.03	0.01	0.01	0.01	0.06	0.45
Germany	0.07	0.02	0.00	0.08	0.12	0.01	0.07	0.30	0.68
UK	0.12	0.02	0.12	0.00	0.09	0.01	0.05	0.28	0.70
France	0.06	0.02	0.17	0.09	0.00	0.01	0.10	0.27	0.71
Canada	0.80	0.04	0.01	0.01	0.01	0.00	0.01	0.02	0.90
Italy	0.07	0.02	0.19	0.06	0.13	0.01	0.00	0.19	0.67
EEC	0.04	0.07	0.30	0.08	0.12	0.00	0.10	0.00	0.72

Source: Adapted from, IMF, Direction of Trade Statistics, 1979, 1996

More importantly, over the long term, as market opening extends to deeper integration behind borders, and involves microeconomic and social policy in the 1990s, the interdependence among G7 members is increasing (Lawrence et al., 1996). As Table 3.12 shows, from the early 1980s to 1994, the share of the stock of G7 member's foreign direct investment (FDI) within the group rose rapidly, particularly after 1990. The largest 1990s gains were not regional but trans-oceanic, as the US-Canada share decreased substantially, the US share to the EU, Germany, France, Italy and, above all, Britain grew, and as Japanese, German, British, French and Italian shares to the US increased.

More broadly, the growth of G7-guided globalization in the 1990 s has increased the exposure of G7 governments and citizens to inflows from abroad of several new human security threats - infectious disease, illegal migration, money laundering and drugs, other transnational crime, and stresses on the environmental (Kirton, 1993). In some cases, such as transnational crime, the sources, recipients and flows of the threats are

Table 3.12   Intra-G7 FDI Stock, 1982-94
(as percentage of total FDI stock)

1982

From/To	US	Japan	Germany	UK	France	Canada	Italy	EEC	Total
US	0.00	0.03	0.07	0.13	0.04	0.21	0.02	0.09	0.60
Japan	0.26	0.00	0.02	NA	0.01	0.02	0.00	0.04	0.35
Germany[a]	0.28	0.01	0.00	0.04	0.07	0.03	0.03	0.26	0.74
UK[b]	0.37	0.01	0.04	0.00	0.03	0.07	0.01	0.08	0.61
France[c]	0.24	0.01	0.07	0.08	0.00	0.02	0.04	0.39	0.85
Canada	0.67	0.00	0.01	0.08	0.01	0.00	0.00	0.03	0.80
Italy[d]	0.12	0.01	0.04	0.04	0.05	0.01	0.00	0.26	0.53

1990

From/To	US	Japan	Germany	UK	France	Canada	Italy	EEC	Total
US	0.00	0.12	0.05	0.06	0.03	0.21	0.02	0.10	0.60
Japan	0.32	0.00	0.06	0.04	0.02	0.02	0.01	0.07	0.54
Germany	0.07	0.03	0.00	0.08	0.13	0.01	0.09	0.32	0.73
UK	0.13	0.03	0.13	0.00	0.11	0.02	0.07	0.27	0.74
France	0.06	0.02	0.17	0.09	0.00	0.01	0.11	0.26	0.72
Canada	0.75	0.06	0.02	0.02	0.01	0.00	0.01	0.03	0.89
Italy	0.08	0.02	0.19	0.07	0.16	0.01	0.00	0.20	0.74
EEC	0.05	0.07	0.33	0.08	0.08	0.00	0.07	0.00	0.67

1994

From/To	US	Japan	Germany	UK	France	Canada	Italy	EEC	Total
US	0.00	0.08	0.09	0.24	0.06	0.16	0.03	0.16	0.83
Japan	0.42	0.00	0.02	0.07	0.01	0.02	0.00	0.07	0.62
Germany	0.21	0.02	0.00	0.09	0.07	0.02	0.04	0.36	0.81
UK	0.32	0.01	0.05	0.00	0.07	0.03	0.01	0.23	0.71
France	0.20	0.00	0.06	0.10	0.00	0.01	0.04	0.37	0.78
Canada	0.52	0.03	0.02	0.10	0.01	0.00	0.01	0.06	0.75
Italy	0.09	0.02	0.06	0.08	0.10	0.01	0.00	0.40	0.75

[a] Data for Germany is 1983 (1982 is not available)
[b] Data for UK is for 1984, (1982-3 is not available)
[c] Data for France is 1987 (1982-6 is not available)
[d] Data for Italy is 1985 (1982-4 is not available)

Source: Adapted from, OECD, International Direct Investment Statistics, Yearbook, 1993-6

largely intra-G7. In many other cases they involve outside members. In all cases, however, it is difficult to envisage autarkic border defenses by G7 members to defend against these new threats to human security. It is the G7 members collectively who alone have the capacity to lead a co-operative international response.

The intervulnerabilities created by cascading G7-centered global-ized interdependence are often dispersed and incremental, and hence politically invisible, in their impact. Proactive and preventative G7 agreement is thus often difficult to achieve. It is only when such process acquires acute attention, urgency and force at times of crisis or shocks that a strong and effective reactive G7 response is forthcoming.

Moreover, effective G7 action is most likely in the face of a second shock - a crisis highly similar to one experienced by G7 members in the proximate past, but to which the G7 did not respond with a coordinated action, with costly consequences for all (Kirton, 1989). It is these second shocks, such as the 1973 and 1979 oil crises, rather than the old consensus of a more than half-century distant depression, war and embedded liberalism, that provide the catalyst and reference point for collective action, and overcome the traditional differences or false new consensus that might otherwise prevail (Putnam and Bayne, 1987; Bergsten and Henning, 1996). Thus, the 1997-8 Asian economic crisis has received a substantially more effective collective response than the 1994 Mexican peso crisis that preceded it.

Common Principles

Reinforcing the ease of communication, consensus formation and co-operation, providing a core reference point and theory for the form co-ordination should take, and offering a powerful catalyst for G7 agreement is the profound reservoir of common principles that G7 members share. The crisis-bred commitment to defend the values of a democratic polity and market economy within the G7's core area, and to extend these principles as the dominant form of domestic governance globally was and is the ultimate raison' d'être for the G7's creation and continuation. These have been reinforced by additional values, such as international openness, human rights, and environmental protection. At present they are further strengthened by a common commitment to providing a floor of social welfare and equity among their citizens in the face of common policy problems, such as the burden on public pension systems caused by aging populations.

Political Control

A final feature fostering high levels of G7 performance is the effective use of the unique feature of the G7 as an institution controlled by popularly and democratically elected political leaders. These features allow leaders to create the cross-issue and cross-regional linkages that create Summit solidarity on the basis of diffuse reciprocity. At the same time, the proliferation of ministerial forums engenders the more detailed management of once domestic but now transnational issues. It further enhances the implementative and surveillance capacity that increases national compliance with leaders' commitments (Kokotsis, 1999; Kokotsis and Kirton, 1997).

Most generally, as in the case of crime and employment, they allow the lateral integration of long separated functions, and, as in infectious disease, the integration of international and deeply domestic practices. The Birmingham model of summit reform promises a major advance in this feature of growing political control with its leaders-only format, prior individual and joint meetings of finance and foreign ministers, both with stand-alone and preparatory agendas, meetings of the ministers with the heads of the three major multilateral organizations, and a serious meeting of G7 leaders immediately prior to the opening of the new G8.

Conclusion

On the eve of the new millennium, there are thus several grounds for concluding that the G7/8 is emerging as the effective centre of global governance for the new era. Its robust recent performance and still unrealized potential are evident in its carefully broadening membership and participation, its comprehensive and flexible agenda embracing subjects once rendered fully domestic by the now porous walls of national sovereignty, and its institutional thickening in ways that involve most domestic department of government and actors from civil society as well. As the Asian financial crisis of 1997 moved in 1998 to highlight the fragility of once tiger-like emerging economies in Asia, the Americas, and post-Soviet Europe, the G7 countries stand out as a bastion of stability, with even beleaguered Japan struggling to escape with only a brief recession no more harmful than that of 1974. With the once "Asian" financial crisis demonstrating the inescapably global rather than geographically regional nature of the new international economy, it is the G7 that is responding collectively to the potential crisis that this deeper intervulnerability, grounded in private sector firms' and banks' practices, now breeds. Despite the immediate difficulties, their response has been directed, notably in Asia and Russia, in forwarding the G7's core principles of democratization with good governance, and transparent, rules-based market economies. And amidst the profound anxieties about globalization now afflicting citizens of the global community, the G7/8 stands virtually alone among international institutions with a vocation for global governance as one where democratically and popularly-elected leaders remain firmly in direct control.

References

Bayne, N. (1995), "The G7 Summit and the Reform of Global Institutions", *Government and Opposition* 30, pp. 492-509.

Bergsten, F. and Henning, R. (1996), *Global Economic Leadership and the Group of Seven*, Institute for International Economics, Washington, D.C.

Commission on Global Governance (1995), *Our Global Neighbourhood: The Report of the Commission on Global Governance*, Oxford University Press, New York.

Daniels, J. (1993), *The Meaning and Reliability of Economic Summit Undertakings, 1975-1989*, Garland Publishing, New York.

De Silguy, Y. (1997), "The impact of the creation of the Euro on financial markets and the international monetary system", address to the Institute of International Finance, Washington, Tuesday, 29 April.

Deibert, R. (1997), *Parchment, Printing and Hypermedia: Communication in World Order Transformation*, Columbia University Press, New York.

Doran, C. (1985), *Forgotten Partnership*, Johns Hopkins, Baltimore.

G7 Research Group (1998a), *The 1997 G7 Compliance Report*, G7 Research Group, University of Toronto (available at www.g7.utoronto.ca), Toronto.

G7 Research Group, (1998b), *The 1998 G7 Compliance Report*, G8 Research Group, University of Toronto (available at www.g7.utoronto.ca), Toronto.

Henning, R. (1996), "Europe's Monetary Union and the United States", *Foreign Policy* 102 (Spring), pp. 83-100.

Ikenberry, J. (1993), "Salvaging the G-7", *Foreign Affairs* 72 (Spring), pp. 132-139.

Ionescu, G. (1995), "Reading Notes, Summer 1995: From International to Global Reform", *Government and Opposition* 30 (Summer), pp. 394-7.

Jayawardena, L. (1989), "World Economic Summits: The Role of Representative Groups in the Governance of the World Economy", *Journal of the Society for International Development* 4, pp. 17-20.

Kindleberger, C. (1973), *The World in Depression, 1929-39*, University of California Press, Berkley.

Kirton, J. (1989), "The Seven Power Summit as an International Concert", Paper presented at the International Studies Association Annual meeting, London, England, April.

Kirton, J. (1993), "The Seven Power Summit and the New Security Agenda", in D. Dewitt, D. Haglund and J.J. Kirton, (eds.), *Building a New Global Order: Emerging Trends in International Security*, Oxford University Press, Toronto, pp. 335-357.

Kirton, J. (1994), "Exercising Concerted Leadership: Canada's Approach to Summit Reform", *The International Spectator* 29 (April-June), pp. 161-176.

Kirton, J. (1995a), "The G-7, the Halifax Summit, and International Financial System Reform", *North American Outlook* 5 (June), pp. 43-66.

Kirton, J. (1995b), "The Diplomacy of Concert: Canada, the G7 and the Halifax Summit", *Canadian Foreign Policy* 3 (Spring), pp. 63-80.

Kirton, J. (1997a), "Canada and APEC: Contributions and Challenges", *Asia Pacific Papers* 3 (May), pp. 1-27.

Kirton, J. (1997b), "Le Role du G7 sur le Couple Integration Regionale/Security Globale", *Etudes Internationales* 28 (Juin).

Kirton, J. (1999), "Economic Co-operation: Summitry, Institutions and Structural Change" in G. Boyd and J. Dunning, (eds.), *Structural Change in the Global Economy*, Edward Elgar, Cheltenham.

Kirton, J. and Kokotsis, E. (1997), "Revitalizing the G-7: Prospects for the 1998 Birmingham Summit of the Eight", *International Journal* 53 (Winter 1997-8), pp. 38-56.

Kokotsis, E. (1999), *Promises Kept: National Compliance with G7 Environment and Development Commitments: 1988-95,* forthcoming Garland Publishing, New York.

Kokotsis, E. and Kirton, J.J. (1997), "National Compliance with Environmental Regimes: The Case of the G7, 1988-1995", Paper prepared for the Annual Convention of the International Studies Association, Toronto, March 18-22.

Labbohm, H. (1995), "G7 Economic Summits: A View from the Lowlands", Netherlands Institute of International Relations, Clingendal, The Hague.

Lawrence, R.Z., Bressand, A. and Ito, T. (1996), *A Vision for the World Economy,* Brookings Institute, Washington, D.C.

Lewis, F. (1991-2), "The G-71/2 Directorate", *Foreign Policy* 85 (Winter), pp. 25-40.

Nye, J. and Keohane, R. (1977), *Power and Interdependence,* Little Brown, Boston.

Odom, W. (1995), "How to Create a True World Order", *Orbis* 39 (Spring), pp. 155-72.

Putnam, R. and Bayne, N. (1987), *Hanging Together: The Seven Power Summits,* Harvard University Press, Cambridge, Mass.

Smyser, W. R. (1993), "Goodbye, G-7", *The Washington Quarterly* 16 (Winter), pp. 15-28.

Ul Haq, M. (1994), "The Bretton Woods Institutions and Global Governance", in Peter Kenen, (ed.) *Managing the World Economy*, Institute for International Economics, Washington, D.C., pp. 409-418.

USTR (1997), United States, United States Trade Representative, Study on the Operation and Effects of the North American Free Trade Agreement, July 1.

Von Furstenberg, G. and Daniels, J. (1992), *Economic Summit Declarations, 1975-1989: Examining the Written Record of International Co-operation,*Princeton University Press, Princeton.

Weintraub, S. (1997), *NAFTA at Three: A Progress Report*, The Centre for Strategic and International Studies, Washington, D.C.

Whyman, W.E. (1995), "We Can't Go On Meeting Like This: Revitalizing the G-7 Process", *The Washington Quarterly* 18 (Summer), pp. 139-65.

Williamson, J. and Miller, M. (1987), "Targets and Indicators: A Blueprint for the International Coordination of Economic Policy", *Policy Analyses in International Economics* 22, Institute for International Economics, Washington, D.C.

4   The G8 and the New Political Economy

MICHAEL R. HODGES[1]

Introduction

The Group of Eight (G8) is not an institution. As Gertrude Stein said of Oakland, there is no "there" there. The G8 is, rather, a process, one which some-times spins off various networks and various initiatives. This role is all well and good. But it is wrong to elevate the G8 to the status of a system of global gov-ernance. It is nothing of the sort. Indeed, if it tries to become such a system, it will destroy itself.

Institutions have clear organizational centres, the most important characteristics of which in practice, are often their cafeterias and pension plans. More importantly, the public's expectation demands that institutions have clear rules, clear criteria for membership, and clearly defined functions. Above all, they should be accountable to somebody. They should ideally be transparent and open. However, if the G8 or the core Group of Seven (G7) acquires these characteristics, it will essentially become useless as an instru-ment for effectively fulfilling its core, and very much needed functions in the international community.

The G7/G8 is a forum, rather than an institution. It is useful as a closed international club of capitalist governments trying to raise consciousness, set an agenda, create networks, prod other institutions to do things that they should be doing, and, in some cases, to help create institutions that are suited to a particular task. Elevating the G7/G8 process into an institution, despite the fact that it lacks the essential features of one, contradicts the original purpose for its creation and raises the danger of snuffing it out (Putnam and Bayne, 1997: 166; Smyser, 1993; Ikenberry, 1993). In doing so the international community would lose one of its most valuable brain-storming sessions. For the G7 is in essence a think tank that counts among its members the individuals who matter most in the world.

The Real Role of the G7/G8

The role of a group such as the G7/G8 should be to raise the consciousness of the international community about new issues. It should also act as a prod where there are indeed suitable institutions to handle existing or new problems. It should then proceed by practising "subsidiarity" by delegating to other organisations the tasks that need to be carried out and moving on itself to other issues. Any other role may well result in an unending increase in the size and responsibilities of the G7/G8 process. Such a proliferation would soon overwhelm it.

The G7/G8 is certainly a very useful bonding process for the leaders of some of the major players in the international community. In mere economic terms its members are the ones who account for the vast bulk of the flow of resources across national frontiers in the world economy. As a result it is useful to have some form of governance of the world economy. But true governance requires structure, rules, accountability and legitimacy in the sense of popular consent. The G7/G8 does not and is not in a position to command any of those critical elements. If one tries to transform this process into an institution it will die. That would be a loss for the world economy.

Reform of the Summit Process

Even with this minimalist conception of a G7/G8 role, and indeed to accomplish these core roles effectively, there is a need for reform of the summit process. In particular, it is useful to make reforms regarding the summit's participation and membership, its agenda, and the formality of the annual gathering.

Participation and Membership

First, it would be useful to have outside guests invited in on an ad hoc basis. Such ad hoc participation could alleviate the sense of exclusion that is manifest in other contemporary arenas, such as Europe's initiative to create a transatlantic marketplace with the US. This transatlantic market place is not going to be realized because the United States is not committed to it. The US is certainly eager to move on regulatory cooperation. It is always very interested in creating plurilateral or multilateral rules as long as they are American rules.

This sense of exclusion is evident elsewhere. The Europeans feel nervous about being excluded from Asia Pacific Economic Co-operation

(APEC). With China's participation in APEC, and the fact that Russia and the United States and Japan are members, why does APEC not invite the European Union to be not merely be an observer at APEC meetings, but to be a full member. This would involve stretching one's sense of geography only a little more than it has already been stretched to justify Russian membership. Such a broadening would be a very good idea and would be far superior to any trans-Atlantic dialogue that can be construed as a zero-sum game that comes at the cost of broader liberalisation initiatives.

In considering the G7/G8 itself, it is quite clear that China is a major player, not only in the regional context of the 1997-8 Asian crisis, but also in the world economy as a whole. China may not be a suitable candidate for membership in a new G9. However, it may be useful to extend formalised links between the G7 or G8 and China, given the growing importance of China to the global economy.

Agenda

A second set of reforms deals with the summit's agenda. At the summit, it is useful to have special themes or topics, if only to remove the temptation to revert to traditional habits such as bashing Japan. Adding special themes or topics to the G7/G8 agenda on an ad hoc basis does present some challenges. In doing so there are dangers of over-burdening the agenda. The current concern with compliance is actually tempting the G8 to revisit issues where it has not been all that successful. One only has to look at the minimal role that the G7 played in the conclusion of the Uruguay Round negotiations, despite the fact that the major players were all members of the G7.

In several successive years the G7/G8 gave a commitment to end the Uruguay Round negotiations by the end of that particular year. They almost always failed to do so. Eventually of course they did conclude the Uruguay Round. This came in part from the positive momentum that the Tokyo summit of 1993 gave to the General Agreement on Tariffs and Trade (GATT) talks (Hodges, 1994: 155). But this came only after many years of the G7 making unfulfilled commitments to act.

Just as there are challenges in adding too much to the G7/G8 agenda, there are problems in having the leaders or their ministers concentrate on too little. The problem of focusing on one subject is demonstrated by the G7 meeting on employment in February 1998. It received almost no media coverage and was not at all exciting. Other problems are inherent in holding an issue specific or limited agenda high-level meeting with heads of state and government. There will be enormous turf battles over which themes are going to be included. There will also be a great deal of nervousness about heads of government discussing just employment or just policing matters, without their respective employment ministers or interior ministers being in very close attendance.

Formality

A wider menu does enable leaders to deal with many issues, to highlight some, and to light fires under civil servants. It does not guarantee a predictable output. However, generating such an assured, concrete output is not the core function of the G7/G8 (Bayne, 1992). If one expects, even with regard to just one issue, that some form of draft treaty will emerge at the end of 48 hours of leader's deliberations, even if these follow ten months of sherpa meetings, one will inevitably be disappointed. It is necessary to lower expectations, cool the temperature and even try to ignore the heads of state and government as they meet. One should let them go off to a country home in an isolated locale and discuss the things they wish to by themselves. Then perhaps one can quite legitimately expect them to do something about the problems that concern us all. But even here they will act within other existing international organisational structures. One cannot expect a "just add water" approach to provide instant G8 solutions to serious problems.

Conclusion

This argument against the institutionalization of the G7/G8 process is that of an idealist and an optimist. If the G7/G8 does not return to focus on its core functions and perform them effectively, it will lose all credibility. It will be correctly identified as essentially an excuse for a shopping trip by journalists. Indeed, at Denver in 1997 the major party for journalists was held in a shopping mall. If the G7/G8 tries to do too much, by behaving as the international institution it is not, then that is what the summits will come to be all about.

Notes

1   It is with great sadness that our colleague and friend passed away

before he was able to fully develop the ideas that he so eloquently shared with us at the Pre-Summit Conference. This chapter is a brief but insightful survey of his observations of the summit process.

References

Bayne, N. (1992), "The Course of Summitry", *The World Today*, February 1992.

Hodges, M. (1994), "More Efficiency, Less Dignity: British Perspectives on the Future Role and Working of the G-7", *The International Spectator* 29 (2), April-June 1994, pp. 141-159.

Ikenberry, J. (1993), "Salvaging the G-7", *Foreign Affairs* 72, pp. 132-139.

Putnam, R. and Bayne, N. (1987), *Hanging Together: Cooperation and Conflict in the Seven-Power Summits*, revised ed., Sage Publications, London.

Smyser, W.R. (1993), "Goodbye, G-7", *The Washington Quarterly* 16, pp. 15-28.

5   G8 Summits and Compliance

ELLA KOKOTSIS AND JOSEPH P. DANIELS

> People and politicians are dominated by quite excessive expecta-
> tions as to what can possibly, or practically, be delivered by gov-
> ernmental economic policies.
> - T.W. Hutchison, *Knowledge and Ignorance in Economics*

Introduction

Since 1975, the leaders of the major industrial democracies have met at the
annual Group of Seven and Group of Eight (G7/G8) summits to address the
most pressing international issues of the day, deliberate on shared problems
and collectively set directions for the global community. The summits have
often produced ambitious and wide-ranging agreements in an effort to generate a multilateral consensus on a diverse number of shared economic and
political issues.

Despite the attention given the G7/G8 summit process and the new
interest by international relations theorists in the issue of compliance with
international agreements (Jacobson and Weiss, 1995; Chayes and Chayes,
1994) there has been little effort to analyze and explain compliance with,
and explore the credibility of, summit policy commitments, and to do so as
a foundation for identifying proposals to improve the summit process.
Although there exists a wealth of scholarly and professional writing on the
G8, virtually all of it focuses on the first order question of reaching agreements through effective policy coordination. Thus, little has been produced
on the soundness of these commitments and the extent to which summit
members comply with them.

Do the G8 summits make a difference? Is the summit process credible and worthy of the enormous media attention it receives? Studies of
summit compliance and credibility indicate that the summits do accomplish
something, but perhaps not as much as one would like them to. Further,
there are significant differences in the compliance record across countries
and issue areas. Reforms suggested here, which would curtail the pomp and
circumstance, streamline the summit format, and narrow the issues dis-

75

cussed to those that meet core criteria for effectiveness, should generate fewer, yet higher quality commitments, which are more likely to be fulfilled.

This chapter details the findings of separate data sets on G7 summit compliance based on studies by George von Furstenberg and Joseph Daniels, Ella Kokotsis, and Ella Kokotsis and John J. Kirton, as well as findings on the soundness of these commitments by Joseph Daniels. It then examines explanations of summit compliance and presents conclusions about why compliance is higher in certain issue areas than in others. It finally offers practical proposals and policy options for the G8 partners to reform the summit process in order to generate higher quality policy commitments that are more likely to be fulfilled.

Gauging Compliance with and the Credibility of Policy Commitments

For past summits to be considered productive and meaningful, and the process viewed as credible, the policy commitments endorsed by the leaders and made public though the summit declaration should meet three criteria. First, they should be ambitious. Second, they should be complied with. Thirdly, the links between means and ends should be based on sound reasoning. Existing evidence is used to examine if the policy promises made at the summits meet these criteria. Doing so casts light on the various conjectures and theories of effective multilateral policymaking. In this manner, the quantitative record of the summits is employed to identify past success and provide insights on how to improve the summit process itself.

Before summarizing various findings about the record of compliance, it is useful to consider the general methodological approach that makes summary scores meaningful. Von Furstenberg and Daniels (1991, 1992) were the first to quantify commitments made at the summits and gauge the extent to which these commitments have been fulfilled. This work, which centers on the economic communique only, establishes a uniform approach for gauging compliance.

Methodological Approach to Compliance Measurement

Arguably, the economic communiqué issued at the conclusion of each summit represents a quasi-legal contract, as the leaders endorse the commitments contained therein. This document is used as the sole data source for the von Furstenberg and Daniels methodology, which ignores statements or press releases that may proceed or follow the release of the communiqué. Peter Hajnal's study, *The Seven Power Summit: Documents from the Summits of Industrialized Countries, 1975-1989*, contains the official economic communique of these early summits and is the source document of these studies (Hajnal, 1989).

There are two general types of commitments that are embedded in the communiqué. The first type is a policy measure, which is a commitment to deliver a specific legislative package, such as a balanced budget agreement. The second type of commitment is a policy outcome, which is a shift in an economic variable, such as reducing the deficit, or reducing inflation. Only those commitments that are concrete enough to identify and quantify the intended policy measure or policy outcome are considered.

The next step in monitoring compliance is to establish a scoring metric that assigns a number reflecting the degree to which a commitment was fulfilled. The classic approach is to define a range of scores from -1 to 1, where a score of 1 reflects complete fulfillment. A score of -1 is assigned if the actual outcome was the opposite of that committed to. Focusing primarily on policy outcomes, von Furstenberg and Daniels use the entire interval between -1 and 1 to assign scores. This methodology enables the identification and quantification of the commitments and assesses in a uniform manner the degree to which they were fulfilled. The scores can then be used to examine various hypothesis regarding the summit process.

Summary of Findings on Compliance

Using the methodology described above, von Furstenberg and Daniels (1992) derive an overall average score for the 209 commitments revealed in the communiqués of the first fifteen summits. The average score was 0.317, or 32 percent, meaning that, roughly one-third of what was promised was actually delivered by the policymakers. These results suggest that G7 members do comply, albeit weakly, with their summit commitments. Moreover, compliance scores vary widely by country, with high compliance coming from Canada and Britain and low compliance from the United States and France. Compliance also varies widely by issue area, with international trade and energy receiving high compliance scores and interest and exchange rate management receiving low scores.

Subsequent research by von Furstenberg and Daniels (1993) combines macroeconomic forecasts generated by the Organization for Economic Cooperation and Development (OECD) with the policy commitments made at the annual summits. Since these forecasts are generated so near the time of the summits, it is reasonable to assume that the forecasts and summit commitments are independent of each other. The forecasts, therefore, can be used to determine the degree of ambition of summit commitments.

Using the 209 commitments of the first study, the authors are able to generate sample statistics to test the joint-null hypothesis of "no summit ambition" and "no summit effect". Again, though the overall score is low, the authors are able to reject, in a statistical sense, the null hypothesis. That is, the commitments are ambitious and there was low, but positive compliance (see Table 5.1). This conclusion stands in stark contrast to the opinion of one sherpa at the 1997 Denver summit, who claimed that the "summits

Table 5.1   Average (a), Standard Deviation (SD) and Number of Scores (N) for 1975-89 Economic Summit Undertakings

Score	Average	SD	N	$(N-1)^{a.5*}$
All Undertakings	0.307	0.684	203	0.070
- with 6A replacing 6.	0.355	0.649	135	0.086
A. By Country, Ordered from Largest, By Size of 1980 GNP				
United States	0.246	0.730	33	0.177
Japan	0.262	0.632	28	0.192
Germany	0.346	0.740	23	0.213
France	0.240	0.612	23	0.213
United Kingdom	0.413	0.743	21	0.224
Italy	0.274	0.688	26	0.200
Canada	0.409	0.603	24	0.209
All Single-Country	0.306	0.685	178	0.075
All Multi-Country	0.314	0.687	25	0.204
B. Detail by Function and Controllability				
1. Real GNP Growth	0.397	0.623	17	0.250
2. Demand Composition	0.233	0.801	7	0.408
3. International Trade	0.734	0.364	7	0.408
4. Fiscal Adjustments	0.259	0.680	40	0.160
5. Interest Rate	0.221	0.526	20	0.229
6. Inflation Rate	0.221	0.731	80	0.113
6A. Multi-Country Scoring	0.266	0.672	12	0.302
7. Foreign Exchange Rate	-0.700	0.301	2	1
8. Aid and Schedules	0.265	0.388	5	0.5
9. Energy	0.660	0.559	25	0.204
Direct Policy Measures	0.279	0.617	10	0.333
All Others	0.309	0.688	193	0.072
All Except Energy	0.258	0.686	178	0.075
All Except Inflation	0.364	0.646	123	0.091

This is the standard deviation (SD) of the average score under the joint null hypothesis that the population value of the SD of scores is 1 because Summit ambition and effect are both 0.

Source: Scores for 1975-80 Summits calculated by George von Furstenberg and Joseph P. Daniels in "Policy Undertakings by the Seven Summit Countries: Ascertaining the Degree of Compliance". Carnegie-Rochester Conference Series on Public Policy 35 (Autumn 1991), 267-308

tend to under-promise and over-deliver".

Subsequent compliance studies, conducted by Kokotsis (1998), and Kokotsis and Kirton (1997), analyze the G7's compliance record from 1988-1995 in regard to the G7's environment and development commitments, which flourished during this period. These studies explore the compliance record of the G8's most and least powerful members, the United States and Canada, in an effort to examine the effects on compliance of overall relative capability and to explore the way differences in national institutions affect compliance outcomes.

Four issue areas critical to the global environment and development agenda - climate change, biodiversity, developing country debt and assistance to Russia - are considered. The period from 1988-1995 provides an era of sustained summit attention to, and important action on these issues. It is a period during which summit attention and ambition has varied, and one where lags in compliance are visible. This combination of eight years, two countries, and four issue areas, including 83 specific commitments, offers enough cases to identify compliance patterns and isolate key compliance variables (see Figure 5.1).

Figure 5.1   A Comparison of U.S. vs. Canadian Compliance with G7 Commitments, 1988-95

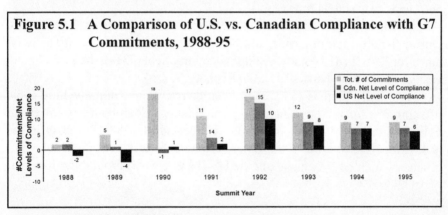

Source: Compiled by E. Kokotsis

These findings suggest that during its third summit cycle, the G7 produced a large number of specific and often ambitious environment and development commitments - 34 regarding climate change, 15 regarding biodiversity, 13 regarding developing country debt, and 21 regarding assistance to Russia. Canadian and U.S. compliance with these commitments has generally been positive, with an overall score of 43%. Yet wide variations appear by country, issue area, and over time: Canada's net score of

53% contrasts with the U.S. net score of 34%. Compliance is much higher in regard to assistance to Russia and developing country debt, than for climate change and above all biodiversity.

These findings suggest several trends. First, during its third seven-year cycle, the G7 offered a larger number of specific and often ambitious environment and development commitments than was the overall norm for the earlier period. These findings thus suggest that the summit has become more active in generating specific, identifiable, and measurable agreements in these key areas.

Second, wide variations arise by country, from Canada's 53% to the U.S.'s 34%. This outcome is consistent with that found by von Furstenberg and Daniels (41% for Canada and 25% for the U.S.). As the methodology of Kokotsis, and Kokotsis and Kirton differs slightly from that of von Furstenberg and Daniels, as the former employ a discrete scale, using only the values of -1, 0 and 1, while the latter use all possible values between -1 and 1, direct or absolute comparisons cannot be made. Hence, no definitive conclusions can be reached regarding rising or falling compliance scores between the periods considered, or for a widening or narrowing of compliance gaps between nations.

Third, there continues to be wide variation across issue areas. During the third summit cycle, compliance is much higher in regard to assistance for Russia (81%) and developing country debt (73%), than for climate change (34%) and, particularly, biodiversity (-13%).

Finally, there is significant variation over time within the third cycle of summitry for G7 environment commitments. Compliance is lower for both Canada and the U.S. in the pre-Rio period of 1988-1991 than in the post-Rio period of 1992-1995. There is a notable peak period of high compliance, which both Canada and the US share, centred around the Rio year of 1992.

Means-Ends Relationships and Credibility of Commitments

Just as the declarations make public the policy promises, they also provide glimpses of what the actions promised are aimed at helping accomplish. In this way, some of the general economic relationships and specific links between means and ends the policymakers subscribe to have come to light, revealing occasional disagreements, shifts of emphasis or evolution of viewpoints over time.

In theory, disagreement among policymakers on the "correct" structure of the economy, and therefore the appropriate policy responses, can present a formidable obstacle to economic policy coordination. It is doubtful that such disagreements are very inhibiting to the policy process, as policymakers are exposed to various models of domestic agencies as well as the models of their foreign counterparts. Thus, a consensus view is developed that incorporates the various modeling ideologies, forecasts, track records, and judgments, all of which are held with varying degrees of conviction. Multiplier and policy lag uncertainty, on the other hand, may indeed inhibit the coordination process. In essence, the viability of economic theory that policymakers subscribe to becomes a "technological constraint" on establishing policymaking credibility (Blackburn and Christensen, 1989).

Daniels (1993) represents the lone comprehensive empirical evaluation of the means-ends relationships advanced at the economic summits. In this study, the various relationships that were revealed in the declarations of the first fifteen summits were inventoried and evaluated in light of recent empirical evidence found in the literature or provided by the author. Based on this evidence, the relationships were judged as either "well-advised", "arguable", or "ill-advised". Further, the relationships were classified as Keynesian, new classical, or other, to determine if there was any progression of economic thinking revealed in the declaration.

Eighteen distinct economic relationships were gleaned from the declarations of the first fifteen summits. The classification of relationships displayed no significant pattern or shift in economic thinking over time. It does, however, show that understandings that relate to national aggregates imply a traditional Keynesian view, while understandings that rest on external linkages are consistent with a Mundell-Flemming model for internal and external balances.

One might suspect that policymakers would play it safe and promote publicly only those actions whose motivation is above challenge, thus reinforcing the credibility of their policy announcements. By comparing the relationships advanced in the declaration with the empirical evidence, this does not appear to be the case. Seven of the eighteen relationships were considered to be "well advised". Ten, however, were considered to be "arguable". Hence, the effectiveness of many of the policy actions announced at the summits may be compromised by the uncertainty of economic theory and models' forecasts that policymakers subscribe to.

To summarize, the G7/8 summits have delivered a large number of policy commitments on economic, environmental, and development issues. The extent to which these commitments were fulfilled is positive, though, in the case of economic commitments, disappointingly low. Further, promises were ambitious, rejecting the notion that policy makers "do not go out on a limb" at the summits. Additionally, the means-ends relationships that policy commitments rest upon are suspect and possibly compromise the effectiveness of the policy actions *even if they were fully complied with*. Thus, the summits are indeed worth something, but leave much room for improvement in the process they currently follow.

Explanations of Summit Compliance

Given that summit declarations are not legally binding documents, that no formal enforcement mechanism exists to ensure that implementation systematically occurs, that domestic circumstances and leadership change from year to year, and that some commitments are superseded by subsequent agreements, one might expect the compliance with G8 summit commitments would be very low. The studies outlined above conclude, however, that over time, the summit has, in general, been active in generating agreements that are specific, identifiable and measurable, that compliance with Summit commitments has been positive and sustained, and that positive compliance appears across countries. How does one account for and explain these patterns of summit compliance?

Conjectures on Policy Coordination

The scores that resulted from the von Furstenberg and Daniels studies described above were grouped by summit, country, function, and controllability (see Table 5.1). The authors use these aggregate scores to draw conclusions on some popular conjectures regarding international policy making. The first conjecture is that joint economic commitments tend to be honored to a lesser degree than an individual commitment, as collective commitments generate "free-rider" problems. The findings indicate no statistical difference between these two types of commitments. Hence, compliance with collective commitments was no less than with commitments assigned to specific countries.

The second conjecture considered is that commitments that promise delivery of a policy measure or instrument that is under the direct control of policy makers would be honored to a higher degree than commitments promising an outcome for a policy target (Putnam and Henning, 1989). The scores reveal the opposite. Commitments on direct policy measures receive a lower than average score than those on economic targets. It appears that policymakers have as much difficulty adopting policy measures as they do forecasting the impact of policy measures on target variables.[1]

Finally, it is argued that policy makers of smaller nations would scrupulously honour their commitments so as to provide political leverage over the policy makers of the larger and more powerful nations. Further, the degree to which one nation can visit macroeconomic externalities upon another depends on the relative size of the nations (Dobson, 1991). As a result, large nations would be less likely to honor their commitments.

Though Britain and Canada received the highest compliance scores, and the United States the second lowest, the scores do not reveal any systematic pattern based on economy size. Likewise, there is no significant correlation of compliance scores with the relative size of the economy, as measured by its GDP. Therefore, the evidence does not support either conjecture relating compliance to the size of the nation.

Institutional Variables and Regimes

Institutional variables and the role of regimes point to further explanations of summit compliance. The findings on debt and assistance to Russia indicate that there has been a sustained, and in fact high level of summit compliance by both Canada and the US in these issue areas during the third summit cycle. This reflects important national institutional variables at work. Within both of these issue areas, the implementation of summit resolutions occurs through long-established departments (Treasury and Finance) possessing well-defined domestic implementation responsibilities, and manifesting strong institutional links to powerful multilateral organizations.

The existence of a well-defined and clearly established process within Treasury and Finance for the domestic implementation of debt and Russian-related commitments helps guarantee a systematic operationalization of the communiqué. Given that finance ministries have the most regularized communication through the G7 finance deputies process, compliance is generally higher with issues stemming from finance ministries, followed by those arising from foreign ministries. This view is confirmed by senior government officials in both Ottawa and Washington who affirm that "finance ministries have the most well-developed coordination of follow-through, with the foreign ministries next".[2] A senior Canadian government official concurred with this correlation between the role of finance ministries with respect to summit compliance:

> On the economic side, it's easier because the institutional frame-
> work already exists. On the political side, there's no mechanism
> for follow-up. Thus the G7 has been less successful in ensuring
> follow-up on non-economic issues in the past. The G7 finance
> deputies process ensures some level of follow-up, more so than
> within foreign ministries.[3]

By contrast, the Department of Environment in Canada and the Environmental Protection Agency in the United States are examples of departments/agencies possessing less of an established process to deal with the implementation of summit commitments. This is primarily because these agencies/departments have been in existence for a relatively shorter period of time.They are bureaucratically less capable of dealing with the domestic implementation of international commitments. Moreover, they possess less money in overall budgetary terms and are thus less influential than older, more established great departments of state or central agencies - such as Finance or Treasury. As such, lower compliance comes with environment commitments than with those arising from departments of Finance and Treasury.

National institutional variables further serve to account for Canada's higher overall record of summit compliance compared to that of the U.S. Within Canada's Department of Foreign Affairs and International Trade (DFAIT), a permanent G8 summit coordination office, staffed with permanent officers, exists to manage, handle, oversee and execute summit undertakings beginning early on in the preparatory process and continuing throughout the year. By contrast, a summit coordination office, or "line office" dealing specifically with G8 undertakings, does not exist at the U.S. State Department, Treasury, or the White House. Although directives are sent out to ministries regarding summit undertakings, the thrust to move these initiatives forward often wanes after the annual summit due to the fact that a central coordinating office does not exist in the US to execute summit resolutions. According to a US government official, "There is no summit coordination office, unlike in Canada, and the energy falls off dramatically post-summit".[4]

International institutional factors also affect summit compliance. Departments of Finance and Treasury possess well-established institutional links to long-existing international fora, including the Paris Club, International Monetary Fund (IMF) and World Bank. These are the institutions responsible for the implementation of Russian assistance and debt-related issues. Because the G7 members are the major shareholders within these institutions, they are able to set the agenda, prompt action and secure agreements on the implementation of these issues. By contrast, domestic environmental departments lack coordinating centres for G7/8-related activity and oversight and rely for international implementation on the fragmented specialized agencies of the United Nations. Here the G7 countries do not possess overwhelming controlling strength due to both institutional characteristics (the one-country-one-vote rule) and underlying issue-specific capabilities and contributions. An overall lower level of compliance is thus assured, especially for commitments which require action by international organizations for their implementation.

Furthermore, the G7 Finance Ministers and Finance Deputies fora, which have existed since 1986, allows the G7 to reinforce the national-international institutional link and intensely monitor the implementation of G7/G8 commitments. The G7 Finance Ministers and Finance Deputies process is more institutionally entrenched than the newer, more "embryonic" and still-evolving G7/G8 environment ministerial forum that emerged only in 1992. Given that the environment ministerials appeared later in the summit system, compliance is expected to be lower with environmental commitments. What should further be noted is that the timing of such ministerials is also relevant to compliance. According to Nicholas Bayne:

> Ministerials which follow fairly soon after the summit are the most helpful in encouraging compliance. The timing of the IMF meetings of finance ministers, three months later, is useful in this regard. Pre-summit ministerials, like those of the environment ministers, can help shape the summit agenda but may not help compliance.[5]

An additional international institutional variable of relevance is apparent in the summit's environment agenda. The empirical findings reveal that there is no net compliance during the period 1989-1991 in either climate change or biodiversity. Beginning in 1992 and onwards, however, there is a high level of sustained environmental compliance. This is primarily due to two factors. First, 1992 marked the launching of a new era in environmental diplomacy with the convening of the United Nations Conference on Environment and Development (UNCED) in Rio de Janeiro, Brazil. Convening just three weeks later in Munich for their annual summit meeting, the G7 leaders agreed on the importance of ratifying the climate change and biodiversity conventions, and stressed the need to implement the decisions embraced. Thus, as the Earth Summit quickly developed into a nested regime, a "Rio effect" is observed, corresponding with a higher level of environmental compliance by Canada and the US with the agreements reached at Rio and endorsed at the G7 Summit.[6]

The 1991/92 "Rio rise" was also coincident with the institutionalization of the G7 environment ministerials, beginning in Germany just prior to the 1992 Munich Summit, and then continuing in Florence, Italy in 1994, Hamilton, Canada in 1995, Cabourg, France in 1996, Miami, Florida in 1997, and Leeds Castle, England in 1998. These G7/G8 environment ministerials have proceeded to endorse the Rio conventions and have emphasized the importance of their continued implementation.

Finally, there is a third institutional variable of relevance. It relates to the expansion of both the preparatory and follow-up phases of the summit. This expansion has led some officials to conclude that the summit process itself has become more institutionalized over the last summit cycle. In turn, this has precipitated an overall rise in compliance by both Canada and the US during the summit's third cycle as compared to the previous two. According to a Canadian official:

> There was an inherent reluctance to institutionalize the process, although I think it's fair to say that over time, there became more frequent meetings after each Summit, and the meetings to prepare for the next Summit began earlier than before. So it became almost a full-time job and certainly became an annual exercise as opposed to a summer event - not only in the preparatory phases, but also in the stock-taking of what had been achieved.[7]

Political Control by G7 Heads of State and Government

In addition to institutions and regimes, the element of political control helps explain compliance with summit commitments. The fact that leaders themselves are present at the summit table seems to ensure that the decisions they reach, and the commitments they make, carry added weight. There are no higher-level bureaucrats at home to whom their decisions are deferred. As a result, when the leaders become personally associated with a summit commitment, it is somewhat different than if that commitment had been produced by a group of ministers. As such, when the Prime Minister and President are directly involved in the creation of the commitment, that fact has a major impact on policy and the priority of policy implementation on the home front. Moreover, when the head of state or government attaches a high degree of personal importance and commitment to certain issues, the degree of implementation is even higher.

This political control variable also takes into account the leader's individual personality and the importance he/she places on international institutions and agreements, including those of the G7/G8 more generally. For example, if a head of state or government demonstrates an attachment to sustainable development initiatives, consistently advances these themes at the annual summits and demonstrates a commitment to multilateralism and the G7/G8 process more specifically, compliance levels will tend to be higher.

Yet because G8 heads are not merely leaders, but democratically-elected ones, their ability to impose their implementing will within their government is constrained by their political standing within society at large. When leaders and their parties enjoy high approval ratings and popularity, their ability to implement is increased. In addition, when domestic public opinion favors a particular issue - such as the environment in both Canada and the U.S. - even unpopular leaders at the time, facing a likely electoral defeat (such as Prime Minister Mulroney and President Bush) will comply with their communiqué commitments. This is primarily because leaders recognize the effects of public opinion and political pressure in areas important to their electorate.

Improving Compliance and the Quality of Commitments

In order for the G7/G8 summits to provide an environment for effective policymaking, they must establish a credible record, or the expectations placed upon them and the attention paid to them will surely fade. The recommendations provided below are primarily based upon an analysis of the evidence cited above, supplemented by material drawn from the general scholarly literature on compliance, monitoring and enforcement. Six proposals for summit reform to enhance compliance and credibility are offered.

First, following British Prime Minister John Major's suggestions for a more streamlined summit in 1992, the summit agenda should become less overloaded, and reflect a more intense focus on only those issues where the G7/8 can make a notable difference. With the mass of intractable problems that has inundated the annual summit agenda, leaders are less able to reach cooperative agreements and understandings on policy matters, let alone attempt to implement concrete strategies to alleviate the problems in the first instance. If leaders continue to attempt to resolve the myriad of issues they are confronted with every year and fail, they risk damaging their reputations and discrediting the summit process.

Second, leaders should internationalize domestic policy issues only when, in the words of Putnam (1989) and Paarlberg (1997) a "positive synergistic linkage" can be developed. The solution is to remove from the agenda domestic issues that are not yet "ripe" as their internationalization may led to negative synergistic linkages, delaying domestic actions and reform.

Third, summit leaders should focus on policy initiatives whose means-ends relationships are well understood and accepted. Leaders should articulate the means-ends relationships so as to establish their credibility and thus maximize their effects on private agents.

Fourth, the G7/G8 should advance commitments in areas where individual leaders and the collective heads of state and government hold "formal" and real "authority". As explained by Aghion and Tirole (1997), formal authority is the right to decide whereas real authority is effective control over decisions. For example, issues of monetary policy have never been, for all practical purposes, on the summit agenda. It was readily understood that most of the leaders had neither the right to decide monetary objectives nor did they exercise control over monetary policy decisions. Loss of fast-track authority by the U.S. President would then imply that trade should not be part of the summit agenda. Likewise, commitments to be fulfilled by supranational organizations should occur where the G7/G8 has a high degree of real authority, such as the IMF, as opposed to organizations in which the G7 does not possess disproportional voting rights, such as the World Trade Organization (WTO).

Fifth, related to issues of real and formal authority and principal-agent problems is the credibility of the underlying institutional body that will develop, implement, and carry out policy. Policy dialogue at the summit level should embrace only those areas where adequate domestic institutional bodies exist to develop and implement domestic policies. Commitments made by principals whose agents are ill-equipped to carry out the commitment can jeopardize the credibility and effectiveness of the policy announcement. In addition, the responsible institutional body should be identified out so that the principal-agent relationship is understood.

Sixth, the 1998 Birmingham summit adopted a format similar to that initially envisaged for the first G7 summit, whereby the leaders meet completely separately from foreign and finance ministers. The importance of leaders meeting on their own during the summit should not be overstated, however. Compliance with summit commitments is more likely to come with ministers on site during the three-day event. This is for three important reasons. First, on-site finance and foreign ministers will generally have a clearer understanding of the context and more specific aspects of the economic and political commitments and will thus be able to suggest appropriate implementation, monitoring and enforcement strategies. Second, with ministers present on site, leaders can immediately instruct them to contribute resources from their respective ministries at the earliest possible stage in the implementation process. Third, ministers can advise heads of state and government immediately of unrealistic commitments and thus prevent them from making commitments that cannot be kept. Thus, in order for compliance with summit commitments to be a realistic objective for the G7/G8 members, it is essential that they return to their previous format of having key ministers on site during the summit itself.

These six suggestions for reform provide a guide as to what issues should be on the summit agenda by explicitly pointing to a more streamlined and focused agenda as well as a more coherent and directed communiqué. The final declarations should result in fewer commitments of higher quality and greater credibility. In this regard, commitments are more likely to be fulfilled when their impact on private agents and ultimate welfare targets are maximized.

Conclusion

It is undeniable that when heads of state and government get together, there is no such thing as "just talk". However, when the summit agenda is filled with idle time and cocktail parties, as the summits have increasingly done, little can be expected. Yet the expectations and attention placed on the summits is high and continues to grow, as evidenced by the increasing number of media credentials issued each year.

Compliance studies indicate that the summits do accomplish something, but perhaps not as much as one would like them to. Reforms that lead to a streamlined and simpler summit format and that narrow the issues discussed to those that meet the criteria suggested above should generate fewer, yet higher quality commitments, which are more likely to be fulfilled. Though what one expects the summit to accomplish may be narrowed, it is more likely that the summits can accomplish something.

Notes

1   Energy is one functional area that stands apart in the von Furstenberg and Daniels studies, indicating that policymakers may be more successful at microeconomic reforms rather than macroeconomic policies.

2   Interview with senior U.S. government official, Washington, D.C., March 12, 1997.

3   Interview with senior Canadian government official, Toronto, February 12, 1997. Note that whereas G7 finance ministers meet four times a year to specifically discuss G7-related matters, foreign ministers meet only once a year, and only on the margins of the opening session of the United Nations General Assembly.

4   Interview with senior U.S. government official, Washington, D.C., March 11, 1997.

5   Interview with Sir Nicholas Bayne, Surrey, England, February 1, 1997.

6   The Earth Summit is referred to as a "nested regime" because of the institutional developments that rapidly transpired vis-a-vis the Rio declarations following the conclusion of the United Nations Conference on the Environment and Development (UNCED) in 1992. For example, the UN Commission on Sustainable Development was established in the aftermath of UNCED as the follow-up body for the Rio conventions. Moreover, permanent secretariats were established for both the Climate Change and Biodiversity Conventions in Bonn and Montreal respectively, with each possessing the institutional underpinnings of a more formal regime: fixed headquarters, a permanent secretariat, budgetary allocations and the creation of binding and enforceable rules.

7   Interview with senior Canadian government official, Montreal, January 31,1997.

References

Aghion, P. and Tirole, J. (1997), "Formal and Real Authority in Organizations", *Journal of Political Economy*, 105(1), pp. 1-29.

Bergsten, C.F., and Henning, C.R. (1996), *Global Economic Leadership and the Group of Seven*, Institute for International Economics, Washington, D.C.

Blackburn, K. and Christensen, M. (1989), "Monetary Policy and Policy Credibility", *Journal of Economic Literature*, vol. 27, pp. 1-45.

Chayes, A. and Chayes, A.H. (forthcoming), *The New Sovereignty: Compliance with International Regulatory Agreements*.

Daniels, J. (1993), *The Meaning and Reliability of Economic Summit Undertakings: 1975-1989*, Garland Press, New York.

Dobson, W. (1991),"Economic Policy Coordination: Requiem or Prologue?" *Policy*

Analyses in International Economics, vol. 30, Institute for International Economics, Washington, D.C.

Hodges, M. (1994), "More Efficiency, Less Dignity: British Perspectives on the Future Role and Working of the G7", *The International Spectator*, 29(2), pp. 141-159.

Jacobson, H.K. and Weiss, E.B. (1995), "Strengthening Compliance with International Environmental Accords: Preliminary Observations from a Collaborative Project", *Global Governance*, vol.1, No. 2, May-August, pp. 119-148.

Kokotsis, E. (1998), *National Compliance with G7 Environment and Development Commitments, 1988-1995*, Ph.D. Dissertation, University of Toronto.

Kokotsis, E., and Kirton, J.J. (1997), *National Compliance with Environmental Regimes: The Case of the G7, 1988-1995*, paper presented at the Annual Convention of the International Studies Association, Toronto, Ontario, March 18-22, 1997.

Mitchell, R.B. (1994), *Intentional Oil Pollution at Sea: Environmental Policy and Treaty Compliance*, MIT Press, Cambridge, Mass.

Paarlberg, R. (1997), "Agricultural Policy Reform and the Uruguay Round: Synergistic Linkage in a Two-Level Game?" *International Organization*, 51(3), pp. 413-44.

Putnam, R. (1989), "Diplomacy and Domestic Politics: The Logic of Two-Level Games", *International Organization*, 42, pp. 427-460.

Putnam, R., and Bayne, N. (1987), *Hanging Together: Cooperation and Conflict in the Seven-Power Summits, 2nd Edition*, Harvard University Press, Cambridge, MA.

Putnam, R. and Henning, C.R. (1989), "The Bonn Summit of 1978: A Case Study in Coordination", in R.N. Cooper, B. Eichengreen, G. Holtham, R.D. Putnam and C.R. Henning (eds.), *Can Nations Agree?* Brookings Institution, Washington, D.C., pp. 12-140.

Smyser, W.R. (1993), "Goodbye, G7", *The Washington Quarterly*, Vol. 16, No. 1, pp. 15-28.

Von Furstenberg, G., and Daniels, J.P. (1991), "Policy Undertakings by the Seven Summit Countries: Ascertaining the Degree of Compliance", Carnegie-Rochester Conference Series on Public Policy, 35, pp. 267-308.

Von Furstenberg, G. and Daniels, J.P. (1992), *Economic Summit Declarations, 1975-1989: Examining the Written Record of International Cooperation*, Princeton Studies in International Finance, Princeton University Press, New Jersey.

Yoshitomi, M. (1995), "Main Issues of Macroeconomic Coordination: The Peso, Dollar and Yen Problems", 35-59, in S. Ostry and G.R. Winham, (eds.) *The Halifax Summit: Issues on the Table,* Centre for Foreign Policy Studies, Dalhousie University, Halifax.

Part II
The Financial Challenges

6 Japan's Summit Contributions and Economic Challenges

KOJI WATANABE   For

FYI

> Summits are by definition tall and therefore can see further,
> further than ministers or bureaucrats

Since the inception of the summit at Rambouillet in France in 1975, the annual Group of Seven (G7) and now Group of Eight (G8) summit has become and remains among the most important diplomatic venues for Japan. Membership in the G7 has constituted symbolic and substantive proof that Japan is a major economic power among the industrial democracies, and that it shares a leadership role in managing and shaping a new world economy.

For a long time the G7 summit was the only annual multilateral gathering attended annually by the Japanese Prime Minister, as Japan was not a member of the North Atlantic Treaty Organisation (NATO), the European Union (EU), nor the Commonwealth. This changed somewhat when the Asia Pacific Economic Cooperation (APEC) forum started holding annual leaders' meetings in 1993 and the Asia-Europe Meeting (ASEM) forum established regular summits every two years. However, the G7/G8 annual summits have retained their singular importance to Japan because they represent a gathering of the leaders of the major industrial democracies that share common global perspectives and a belief in the values of democracy and the market economy.

The Summit's Origin and Evolution

Central to the origin of the G7 in the middle of the 1970s was the change in the relative strength of the United States, due to the trauma of Vietnam, and the concomitant rise of Japan and Western Europe. The world was then marked by an East-West political divide and by a North-South economic divide. Despite the Sino-Soviet rivalry and the emergence of the Organization of Petroleum Exporting Countries (OPEC), this essential twofold divide persisted throughout the 1970s and 1980s.

In the 1990s the collapse of the Soviet Union caused the East-West divide to disappear. In addition, the North-South divide became blurred with the rise of an economically dynamic group of developing countries, particularly those in East Asia. China itself was becoming an economic and military power center during this period.

To what extent and in what manner have the summits contributed to this global transformation of the last quarter century? The answer is partly found in the list of major agenda items of the last 23 summits. These are: first and foremost, non-inflationary growth; monetary issues; trade; energy; north-south issues; and east-west relations. To these were subsequently added: environment; terrorism; drugs; money laundering, transnational crime; and infectious diseases. Alongside the economic and global issues that were and still are of common concern among the summit leaders, there have been a host of political issues that were of immediate importance for the summit participants at the time of each summit. These have included Afghanistan, the Falklands, Intermediate-Range Nuclear Missiles, the Iraq/Iran conflict, Tianamen Square, the North Korean nuclear issue, and the ongoing crisis in the former Yugoslavia, including Bosnia.

The challenge presented by the break-up of the Soviet Union and the constantly re-occurring cycle of crisis in Russia has been among the most important and tangible case of policy coordination organised through the summit process. This process eventually led to Russian President Boris Yeltsin's participation in the annual meetings of the summit leaders. It is one policy area where Japan has been involved in a unique manner. In sum, the Russian issue is a specific instance of the G7/G8 summit's positive contribution to global governance.

The Summit and Economic Growth

Among economic issues that have been dealt with in the summit process, the first and foremost has always been the subject of growth and employment. The very objective of the first summit of Rambouillet of 1975 was "to assure recovery of our economies and to reduce the waste of human resources involved in unemployment". To assess the track record of the summit contribution to the economic growth of the world economy in general, and to economies in North America, Western Europe and Japan in more specific terms, is difficult.

Summit Declarations in the past described the economic perform-ance of the 1980s in a positive manner. The Toronto summit Declaration of June 1988 says:

> We observed a large contrast between the 1970s and 1980s. The former was a decade of high and rising inflation, declining pro-ductivity growth, policies dominated by short term considera-tions and frequently inadequate policy co-operation.

In the 1980s inflation has been brought under control, laying the basis for sustained strong growth and improved productivity. The result has been the longest period of sustained growth in post-war history. As it turned out, the G7 economies enjoyed stable growth from 1983 to 1990 and suffered recession in 1991 and 1992. Recovery started again in 1993 with the United States, Canada and the United Kingdom leading the way.

The Economic Declaration of the Tokyo summit of 1993 and that of Naples of 1994 described the economic landscape from the summit in an appropriate way. The 1993 Declaration said:

> We are concerned about insufficient growth and inadequate job creation in our economies. Recovery is continuing in North America but remains modest, Europe is still in a marked reces-sion although there are some signs of recovery. Japan's econo-my is over the worst and some recovery is now in sight.

The Declaration of 1994 said:

> A year ago recovery was absent or hesitant in all our economies. Today encouraging results are emerging, recovery is under way. New jobs have been created and in more and more of our economies people are getting back to work.

Hence, the summit declarations turned optimistic once again

The Changing Japanese Economy

Amidst this change in the global economy in the 1980s and early 1990s the Japanese economy encountered difficulties with which the summit had to contend. By 1996 the Japanese were not unhappy about their life in Japan, but were uneasy about the future. By the spring of 1998 the Japanese were still not unhappy about their current condition, but were more uneasy and some even apprehensive about the future.

The Japanese became uneasy about the future because they increasingly realized that the socioeconomic system that had worked so well for them had ceased to function as before. That system has been geared to attain two national objectives. One was growth, by catching up with the United States. The other was democracy, by creating a wealthy, egalitarian society centered upon the protection of the weak.

That system had two main features. The first was Japan's industrial structure, which had been developed in the catch up phase. It was characterized by the juxtaposition of both high and low productivity sectors. The former were represented by rapidly expanding export industries such as automobiles, electronics and machine tools. The latter were represented by regulated or protected sectors such as agriculture, banking and finance, real estate and the non-tradable, largely service sectors of distribution, construction, domestic transportation, communication and utilities. The rapid expansion in exports of products from high productivity sectors such as automobiles,   electronics, and semiconductors brought about an appreciation of the yen. This appreciation also reflected the failure of increasing imports to expand to a commensurate degree. Thus Japan emerged as a structurally high cost economy.

The second feature, very much at the centre of the system, was the bureaucracy. Views differ as to the extent to which the bureaucracy contributed to the high-speed development of the Japanese economy. However, the bureaucracy in Japan has undeniably played a central role in maintaining political stability under the Liberal Democratic Party (LDP). This regime lasted thirty-eight years from 1955 until 1993 and returned to power again in 1996.

In particular, the bureaucracy played a distinctive role in protecting and promoting the interests of low productivity sectors of the economy and thus, by extension, serving the interests of the LDP. These low productivity sectors possessed considerable political power through the votes of workers in agriculture, construction, distribution, banking and financing, and small and medium sized enterprises. At the same time, those bureaucracies engaged in protecting the weak in their own domains have been proud and morally motivated as upholders of social justice. They operated with a sense of mission in a manner analogous to that of the continental European social democrats. In effectively doing so they pre-empted the domestic position of the Socialists, the major opposition polit-ical party to the LDP. The prevailing perception had long been that the Japanese bureaucracy was well informed, capable, clean, hard working, and dedicated to carrying out state functions. The high degree of confi-dence in the bureaucracy, shared among business, politicians and the gen-eral public, was a very important factor for stability.

The system worked well through the 1980s and in the process delivered impressive results. Japan's per capita Gross National Product (GNP) rose to a level among the highest in the world. Japan became, as a consequence, the world's second largest economy, following only the United States. By 1990, Japan's labor productivity had caught up with that of the United States. The Japanese also became rich in terms of savings, with the aggregate amount of household savings reaching 1,200 trillion yen, or $9 trillion.

The unemployment rate, even after rising to 4.1% by April 1998, remained among the lowest in the industrial democracies. Japan was among the safest countries to live in. Its environmental problems were brought under control. Japan in the 1990's became the largest donor of economic assistance to developing countries, contributing $14.5 billion a year by 1995. Moreover, Japan was the most egalitarian society among the G7 or G8 countries in terms of income distribution. This was due to a rather flat salary scale and, more importantly, to a very progressive income tax and inheritance tax regime. The highest income tax rate is 65%.

Entering the 1990s, the Japanese discovered that their situation had changed drastically. They realised rather belatedly that their system was in trouble. Since 1992, the Japanese economy registered, in the words of the Organization for Economic Co-operation and Development (OECD), "a strikingly exceptional low growth rate" of less than 1% for three consecutive years. This was in spite of huge fiscal stimuli offered in the form of public works expenditures and special tax reductions.

As a result of this fiscal stimulus over a period of six years, and due to a stagnant economy that caused a shortfall of tax revenue, the annu-al budget picture deteriorated dramatically. The national debt position became one of the worst among the G7 countries. It was shocking to see that Japan, whose fiscal position was considered the most sound among G7 in 1991, had become among the worst. As a point of comparison, the country was unable to meet the 3% ratio of deficit to GDP nor the 60% ratio of debt to Gross Domestic Product (GDP) set by the Maastricht

Treaty. In fact, the Fiscal Structural Reform Act, passed by the Diet in November 1997, had stipulated that the deficit be cut to 3% by Fiscal Year (FY) 2003.

The Causes of Japanese Economic Change

Six factors caused this unprecedented economic stagnation in Japan. Two of these are related directly to the financial bubble and bust. Three others are structural trends. One is psychological.

The first factor was the adjustment following the huge investment in the bubble period of the late 1980s, an investment spree that resulted in excess productive capacities.

The second was the balance sheet effect of bursting that huge bubble. It came in the form of a deterioration of the asset value of stocks and land. This constraining effect persisted, like a body blow in a boxing match, but in a more damaging way and for a much longer time than generally assumed.

The third factor was the appreciation of yen that started in 1986, progressed steadily until 1992 and then rose precipitously until the spring of 1995. Yen appreciation, reflecting a continuous sizable current account surplus and a high cost economy, prompted manufacturing industries to shift a sizable portion of their production abroad, not only to the United States and Europe, but also to Southeast Asia. Japanese direct foreign investment surged, giving rise to apprehension about its hollowing out effect on the Japanese economy.

A fourth factor was the wave of globalization that favored the US economy and also, so it seemed to many, the new emerging economies of South East Asia. At the same time Japan was behaving with irrational exuberance in its bubble economy, basking in asset inflation, complacently believing that it had finally caught up with the United States and enjoying being called "Number One". Furthermore, East Asian countries, including Korea and China particularly, seemed to be catching up as well. Meanwhile, the US economy was in fact forging ahead in developing new information technologies and getting ready to ride the wave of globalization.

Fifthly, the difficulties associated with a rapidly aging society suddenly dawned upon the Japanese. The implications seemed all the more poignant in the aftermath of the bursting of the economic bubble when a decline in the wealth of the nation seemed probable. While life expectancy for both men and women in Japan is the highest in the world, and in itself an impressive achievement, when juxtaposed with the fact that the fertility rate among Japanese women is among the lowest in the world, it presents a most serious challenge.

The sixth factor was a mind-set of inertial optimism. Ever since the bubble burst, both the government and business, particularly those in financial circles, assumed that the Japanese economy would naturally return to a secular growth path and resume what the Japanese call "right shoulder upward" growth. This was the trend that had characterized Japanese economic performance ever since 1945. Based upon that assumption, the government poured trillions of yen into the economy. The Bank of Japan introduced and maintained the lowest official discount rate in history, a rate of 0.5%. Bankers believed that with this support and the resumption of growth that would follow, the malaise of the balance sheets, including that of non-performing loans accumulated through the boom and bust period, would correct itself in due course.

The Drama of 1997

This mind-set played a crucial and unfortunate role in the drama of 1997, a drama that extended into 1998 and beyond. The drama of 1997 started with the general election of October 1996 in which every political party stressed the importance of "reform". That reform became the buzzword in this election reflected the prevailing feeling that the Japanese system was not functioning well. Many felt it was probably in trouble following the boom and bust years and had now entered a prolonged period of stagnation.

But the critical backdrop to the drama was the fact that the economy was finally improving. After three years of stagnation, the GDP growth rate for 1995 came in at a decent 1.5%.[1] The yen hit a peak in the spring of 1995 and then started to depreciate. Most importantly, the economy seemed to be doing very well in 1996, with private investment regaining momentum and personal consumption showing growing strength. Indeed, the real GDP growth rate for 1996 was 3.9% , the highest among the G7 countries that year.

The LDP, led by Prime Minister Hashimoto who had been in power for ten months since January 1996, won the election but failed to achieve a majority. Mr. Hashimoto's slogan for the election campaign was reform, particularly administrative and fiscal reform, as well as financial, economic, welfare and educational reform. Having been finance minister in the early 1990s, Hashimoto wished to put the emphasis on fiscal reform, as the fiscal position had deteriorated a great deal compared to what he had been familiar with.

With the economy picking up, in a seemingly robust manner in the early spring of 1997, the Hashimoto cabinet embarked in April 1997 upon fiscal reform with a vengeance. A tight fiscal policy took shape in multiple ways. The consumption tax rate was raised from 3% to 5% as previously scheduled and a special income tax reduction that had been in effect for two years was abolished. Public works expenditures were to be reduced and the patients' share of medical insurance payments augmented. In total, the budget for FY 1997 beginning April 1st had the effect of extracting from the economy as much as an estimated 9 trillion yen, representing around 2% of overall GDP.

As it turned out, the forces propelling the recovery proved not to be very strong. While personal consumption and housing starts were expected to be affected somewhat by the rise of the consumption tax, the actual dampening effect was much greater. However, it was not until November that the mood changed qualitatively for the worse. The government as late as July 1997 was so confident about the strength of the economy that it embarked upon an unprecedented effort to cut budget spending for the coming three years. Public works expenditures were slated to be cut by 7% and official development assistance by 10%. Defense expenditures were frozen. The government committed itself to introducing the Fiscal Structural Reform Act (FSRA).

In November 1997, personal consumption started to plummet. This was followed by a fall in private investment. Four factors led to this unexpected development. The most dramatic was the bankruptcy of both the largest bank in Hokkaido and the fourth largest brokerage firm, Yamaichi Securities. These developments were shocking, as they destroyed the firmly held myth that large Japanese financial institutions would never go bankrupt. Secondly, financial scandals involving Ministry of Finance officials in charge of banking and securities came to light. Confidence in the bureaucracy in general and the Finance Ministry in particular was deeply shaken. Thirdly, the Asian currency crisis started in July in Thailand. It soon spread to Indonesia and South Korea, and to a lesser extent to Malaysia and the Philippines. At the end 1997 South

Korea was on the verge of a wholesale default. Fourthly, in the face of the declining value of Tokyo stock exchange prices, as well as continuing stagnation in real estate values, banks started to drastically contract their loans in order to qualify for the capital-adequacy standard of the Bank for International Settlements (BIS).

These four factors had a decisive dampening effect on the Japanese economy, multiplying the effect of the restrictive fiscal measures introduced in April 1997. Confronted with the unfolding and unexpected drama of 1997, the government announced a series of financial measures. These consisted of a special income tax reduction of 2 trillion yen for 1997 and a financial stabilization package that could potentially amount to 30 trillion yen. Furthermore, on April 24, 1998, the government introduced a huge fiscal stimulus package amounting to 16 trillion yen, including a tax reduction and additional public works expenditure. As the Japanese GDP is 500 trillion yen, the packages are likely to be large enough to boost GDP by at least by 1 to 2%.

The critical objective thus became the implementation of this package as quickly as possible in order to restore confidence among consumers, business, and the general public. A consensus seemed to be emerging among politicians, businesspeople and in government circles that the stabilization of the banking sector should be the primary objective and that the problem of non-performing loans needed to be resolved.

The Japanese banking sector has always been strictly regulated by the Ministry of Finance. Despite their huge assets, reflecting the high savings of Japanese households, Japanese banks are not competitive. They have not been exposed to competition, regulated as they have been in the form of a "convoy" system. They acted exuberantly in the boom period and are subsequently suffering a bust due to non-performing loans. The fact that the banks are not functioning well as financial intermediaries is a critically important factor hindering Japanese economic recovery. This is now fully recognised. The urgent need for reform became all the more apparent as the Japanese government committed itself to carry out a Japanese "Big Bang" financial liberalization beginning in April 1998. The important policy question became whether the Japanese government was carrying out a stabilization policy for the sake of stability in and of itself or for reform. The political question that remains unanswered is whether to "bail out" the banks or let them "drop out".

The Role of the Summit in the Current Crisis

How does the summit concept or process relate to these Japanese difficulties, which have global implications in light of the currency and financial crisis in some East Asian countries? Could the summit process have done something so that the difficulties that Japan has been facing could have been dealt with differently?

Macro economic policy coordination is important, but there are limits as to its effectiveness. This is due to three factors. Firstly, macroeconomic policy coordination presupposes an effective multilateral surveillance system that allows members to share sufficient knowledge of the political as well as economic dynamics of the country concerned. Secondly, summit coordination tends to be, and has to be, centered on those economic policy issues that are more relevant to external balances. Thirdly, since the economy is affected by a psychology of optimism and pessimism, the effect of political messages emanating from the summit can be rather perverse.

Did the summit raise any effective warning about the possibility of a bust when the Japanese economy was basking in a period of asset inflation? Japan was praised by its G7 partners for managing to cut the current account surplus to a level of 1.1% and GDP growth rate to 5.6% in fiscal 1990, the peak of the bubble. In fact, the Houston summit economic declaration in July 1990 says:

> In recent years, substantial progress has been achieved in promoting a strong world economy through sound macro economic policies and greater economic efficiency. External imbalances have been reduced in the United States and Japan, whereas in other cases they have increased.

The difficulties that Japan faces as the new millennium approaches are the product of a shift in psychology from inertial optimism toward a sudden loss of confidence. Related to this shift are exchange rate fluctuations. The yen continued to appreciate from 1986 until the spring of 1995 and then began to depreciate. The value of the yen is a psychological barometer of confidence. To the extent that Japan's economic recovery is important for the world economy in general, and for Asian countries in particular, a renewed concerted effort could usefully be encouraged to stabilize the exchange rate of the yen. This is an option the summit can and should explore.

The prevailing feeling both within and outside Japan is that its government should have acted more promptly. But there are understandable political circumstances, if not justifiable circumstances, to explain why the banner of fiscal reform could not be unfolded more rapidly. The important thing, with a very large growth package involving real money presented by the Japanese government in 1998, was that the Birmingham summit welcomed and valued this serious effort. This endorsement should make a substantive difference in providing the much needed confidence required to spur growth.

Finally, if the summit is tall and can see further, it should explore the emerging monetary landscape of the world economy. With the introduction of the Euro and the recent lessons of the Asian currency crisis, questions regarding the value and role of the yen must be considered. This is a subject that will increasingly be discussed in Japan.

Note

1   Statistics are from the publication "Japan", Bank of Japan, Research and Statistics Department, *Economic Statistics Monthly* 614 (May 1998), OECD Main Economic Indicators.

7 Supervising the International Financial System

JOSEPH P. DANIELS (G-8)

F02
G15

Introduction

As the Group of Eight (G8) evolves, the elite club has shown that it is willing to tackle issues that are domestic in nature yet have an international linkage. That is, domestic issues that share a commonality across member nations or have considerable externalities become part of the agenda. Issues of aging populations and employment levels are examples. On the other hand, the G8 has also shown a preference to delegate to international bodies international issues that may affect member nations to varying degrees.

In many cases, the delegation of responsibility is wise. In the case of infectious diseases, developing an agenda and delegating responsibilities to the World Health Organization (WHO) is a sound managerial decision. Delegating agendas and responsibilities to international organizations that are ill-equipped or unable to deal with pressing issues, however, is at best ineffective and perhaps even reckless.

Recent responses of the G8 to contemporary economic problems, which are rooted in the financial sector as opposed to the real sector, have been to ignore, minimize, and delegate to the International Monetary Fund (IMF).[1] The outcome is ineffective and reckless policymaking. In the middle of the financial meltdowns in Asian and Russia, and with contagion lapping at the shores of Latin America, a single day's editorials in the Wall Street Journal argued the following:

> … Argentina is about the only nation where the (International Monetary) Fund's gotten it right since the current crises began with the Mexican bailout back in 1994... The issue is not simply the large amount of money, but also an IMF record that in any responsible financial institution would require the firing of senior management...[2]

In the same article George Soros made the following remark about the response of the G7 nations to the crisis:

The third major factor working for the disintegration of the global capitalist system is the evident inability of the international monetary authorities to hold it together. IMF programs do not seems to be working. The
response of the Group of Seven industrialized countries to the Russian
crises was woefully inadequate, and the loss of control quite scary.[3]

By not handling the recent financial crises in a timely or effective
manner, the G8 has demonstrated that, either by choice or by inability, it is not
an institution of effective global leadership in the areas of deepest importance.
Important issues of financial bailouts and coordination of supervision and regulation must be resolved prior to the new millennium.

Section 2 of this chapter examines the dramatic increase of capital
flows to developing economies and the importance of financial intermediaries in channeling these funds. Section 3 outlines the various risks brought
about by greater integration of capital and money markets. Section 4 presents views on government regulation of domestic financial systems and considers the capacity of existing international organizations to fulfill this role.
Section 5 outlines the critical responsibilities of the Group of Seven (G7)
and G8 in light of 1997-98 financial crises. Section 6 offers a conclusion.

Evolution of Capital Markets

During the Bretton Woods System, capital flows were relatively limited.
Hence, most capital flows and foreign exchange transactions occurred to
finance and facilitate transactions in the real sector. As a result, a typical international payments crisis was a slowly developing payments imbalance driven
by transactions in the real sector. Bretton Woods institutions such as the IMF
and the World Bank were relatively well equipped to deal with these types of
crises.

Following the advent of a floating exchange rate system, most of
the industrialized nations began to remove capital restrictions and deregulate
their domestic monetary and financial markets, beginning with the United
States and Canada in the early 1980s. The daily volume of foreign
exchange transactions mushroomed from approximately $15 billion in
1973 to $1.4 trillion in 1998, a volume that is several times larger than the
daily volume of transactions that occur in the real sector. In addition, cross-
border transactions of bonds and equities in the United Sates (U.S.)
increased from 9 percent of Gross Domestic Product (GDP) in 1980 to 164
percent in 1995 (Daniels and VanHoose, 1999, p. 174).

Increased Capital Flows to Developing Economies

Arguably more important has been the increased volume of capital flows among nations. Indeed, the most striking feature of the 1990s, is the increased volume of capital flows to the emerging countries. Figure 7.1 illustrates the rise in total net private capital flows for the emerging economies, distinguishing between net direct investment flows and portfolio flows. As shown in the figure, net private capital flows to the emerging economies has risen a dramatic 415%.

Figure 7.1 Net Private Capital Flows to Emerging Economies, 1990-96

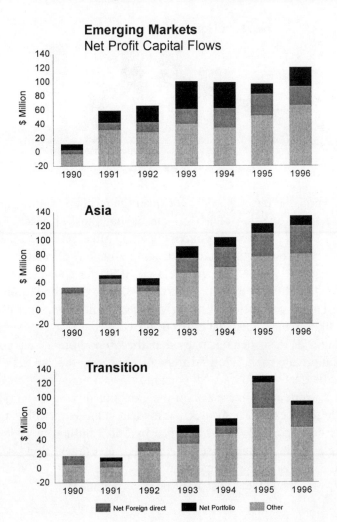

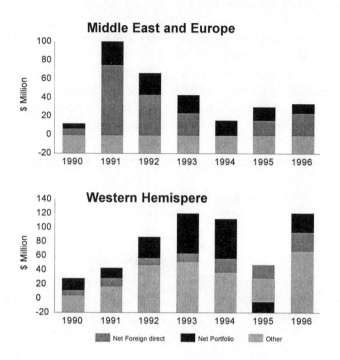

As learned in the 1994-1995 Mexican financial crisis, it is important to recognize the proportion of net private capital flows that are portfolio investments. This flow of short term capital, often referred to as "hot money", can reverse direction quickly, leaving a nation's financial sector in an illiquid position. (See Chang and Velasco, 1998, for an excellent review of the Asian liquidity problem.) Figure 7.1 shows that for the emerging nations, the largest proportion of net private capital flows was net portfolio flows until the Mexican financial crises occurred.

Figure 7.1 also demonstrates that the proportion of net portfolio flows to total private capital flows differs widely across the various regions. For the Middle East and Europe, net portfolio flows account for 42% of total private flows, while it is a mere 8% for the transitional economies. The fact that portfolio flows can reverse quickly is evident in the Western Hemisphere region, where net portfolio flows dropped by $68.3 million in 1995 alone, representing a 112% decline. Net direct foreign investment flows as a per-cent of total net private flows range from 58% for the transitional economies to a scant 7% for the Middle East and Europe economies.

The Importance of Financial Intermediation

It is important to recognize that the capital flows described above are the savings of one nation's residents being loaned to another nation's residents. Financial intermediaries play an extremely important role as they channel these savings to borrowers and help finance domestic investment. The solvency of a nation's intermediaries is critical for the stable flow of capital and continued growth and prosperity.

Unfortunately, history has shown that financial systems and intermediaries are quite fragile. The IMF estimates that since 1980, 133 of the 181 member nations have experienced banking problems considered to be significant (Lindgren, et al, 1996). According to available estimates, the cost of the 1977 through 1985 crisis in Spain amounted to 17% of its output. In the Nordic countries, the costs of the banking crises that occurred in the late 1980s and early 1990s amounted to 8% of Finland's output, 6% in Sweden and 4% in Norway. The cost of the savings and loan crisis in the United States totaled at least $200 billion, or 3% of U.S. output (Goldstein and Turner, 1996).

The banking crises in the developing nations have tended to be much more severe. It is believed that the costs of the 1980's banking crises in Argentina equaled one-half of the nation's GDP. The Mexican crisis amounted to a loss of 12 to 15% of output. The costs of the 1997-98 crises will be considerable. The 1995 real estate collapse in Japan resulted in the nonperformance of more than $250 billion in bank loans. In South Korea more than 10% of all bank loans were non-performing by 1998. For India and China the number of non-performing loans are estimated to be nearly 20% of outstanding loans.

As one might suspect, given the increase in international capital flows, over 354% from 1986-98 (Daniels and VanHoose, 1999), very few nations' capital investment projects are purely financed by domestic intermediaries. Even investment in the United States that is bank-financed increasingly relies on foreign banks, as the largest U.S. corporations use, on average, the services of foreign banks more than domestic institutions. Given the heightened level of integration, a nation's system of intermediaries is now exposed to new sources of risk.

New Sources of Risk

The growth and globalization of capital markets has brought about a vast number of new opportunities for savers and borrowers. It has also generated new risks. There are five particular sources of risk examined here; 'hot money' flows, systemic risk, contagion, increasing sophistication of financial instruments, and regulatory arbitrage.

Hot Money Flows

As demonstrated in the previous section, there has been a dramatic increase in short-term portfolio flows, particularly to the emerging economies. Many of these emerging nations have financial and banking sectors that are under-developed, not regulated, and not properly supervised. When positive, these net inflows can put upward pressure on a nation's currency and on domestic inflation. On the other hand, they also represent a lower cost form of financing (hence lower interest rates) and stimulate a nation's economy.

Portfolio flows can, however, reverse direction at rates that quickly exhaust the cumulative buildup of years of inflows. In an economy with an underdeveloped financial sector, these outflows may result in an illiquid banking system and put downward pressure on the nation's currency. Under a fixed exchange rate regime, the government is faced with opposing problems: The banking system needs additional liquidity while the exchange rate regime requires higher interest rates. This is the type of problem seen in the 1997-98 financial crises (see Glick, 1998, for a survey of the literature in this area).

Herstatt Risk

A second aspect is Herstatt Risk or credit risk that spans borders and/or time zones. In 1974, German banking regulators closed the failed Herstatt bank at 3:30 p.m., after the bank had received European foreign exchange payments but before it made required payments to U.S. banks. Because U.S. banks did not receive anticipated payments, they were, in many cases, unable to fulfill their own obligations. By the time the entire event unwound, U.S. banks had lost as much as $200 million dollars.

Transmission of Shocks

A third aspect of increased globalization is the transmission of shocks and the potential of contagion. As financial markets become more integrated, the transmission of shocks becomes possible and can even be magnified. Such was the case of the U.S. stock market crash of the 1980s. Because of inter-twined markets, the crash spilled into exchanges across the globe. The recent East Asian crises shows that currency crises may have the potential for regional contagion. Empirical work by Glick and Rose (1998) indicates that currency crises affect "clusters" of nations through international trade channels.

Increased Sophistication of Financial Instruments

As the financial markets have evolved, new and highly sophisticated financial instruments have been introduced. The use of these instruments often becomes widespread before appropriate domestic regulators and corporate managers fully understand their risks and benefits. The 1995 collapse of Barings bank illustrates this point. The same day that Peter Baring had to ask the Bank of England to intervene, and the day after the trader involved in the derivatives fiasco, Nick Leeson, faxed in his resignation, Barings was to announce and award company bonuses, including a bonus to Leeson in the amount of £450,000. The total losses to Barings is estimated to be £927 million.

Regulatory Arbitrage

A final aspect, one that has not received as much attention in the literature, is the impact of increased globalization, competition, and technological advances on bank structure. Regulatory arbitrage, establishing foreign offices to avoid domestic regulation, has increased dramatically due to technological advances in banking. Globalization and competition has led to increased merger activity and the creation of "mega" banks. Both activities undermine the attempts of sovereign governments to regulate and supervisor national banking institutions.

　　　The various risks listed above heighten the importance of a sound payments system and a sound system of banks and financial intermediaries. Financial solvency is, therefore, a key policymaking issue and critical to the operation and stability of the global economy.

The Regulation and Supervision of Financial Systems

How should sovereign governments and international organizations respond to the risks of increasing financial integration? It is important to first distinguish between international financial liberalization and financial regulation. Liberalization is the opening up of the financial market to foreign participants, increasing competition and opportunities for domestic banks. Regulation is the governing of the financial sector in order to improve its operation of financial intermediation. Obviously, and as evident in the 1997-98 financial crises, appropriate regulation and supervision is required for the domestic financial system to absorb and channel in an economically efficient way the inflows and outflows of capital.

Views of Government Intervention

One view of government intervention in the financial sector is that financial intermediation is inherently an unstable business whose fortunes rise and fall with the business cycle and that financial markets may have inherent imperfections. Hence, government regulation and safety nets are required to prevent periodic banking collapses.

In line with this view, Von Hagen and Fratianni (1998) identify three main reasons for financial regulation. The first is that small depositors find it too costly to continuously monitor the activities of intermediaries. Hence, small depositors need protection from the risk of bank failure. The second is that regulation is required to prevent large withdrawals from one bank which might affect the entire industry, that is, to prevent contagion. The final reason is to preserve the integrity of the payments system. The authors assert that these types of banking regulation involve the reallocation of risk and therefore wealth among market participants. In a global setting this reallocation can become quite complex as sovereign governments wish to protect domestic residents over foreign residents.

Another view is that regulation that eliminates competition and the existence of safety nets creates a moral hazard problem and may actually be responsible for recent banking crises. This second view has been used extensively to build a critical case against the necessity of international organizations such as the IMF. It has played particularly well on the floor of the U.S. Congress who delayed approval of a new allocation of funds to the IMF until October 1998.

Regulation and Supervision: New or Old Institutions?

In spite of recent criticism, there have been a number of well placed initiatives and actions taken in response to the risks described above. Examples are the Lamfalussy Report, a 1990 Group of Ten (G10) initiative that outlined the legal responsibilities of any intermediary undertaking a large volume wire transfer, the Basle Capital Accord for capital adequacy standards, cross-border banking principles for consolidated supervision, risk management guidelines for derivatives trading, and core principles for effective banking supervision.

Many of these initiatives resulted from G7 directives. The Halifax and Lyon summits, in particular, addressed the global financial situation. (See the excellent volume by Kenen, 1996, where most of the following information is taken from.) Directives to the IMF included a request to the IMF to develop procedures to provide faster access to IMF credit with strengthened conditionality, to develop standards for data availability, and to intensify surveillance beyond Article IV policy reviews. The response was an emergency financing mechanism, the Special Data Dissemination Standards, and publication of Article IV reviews for those countries wishing the reviews to be public.

The G10 was asked to double the credit facilities available to the IMF and to review procedures that might prevent or resolve financial crises. The G10 responded with a new arrangement that doubled available IMF credit and, as a first-step, conducted a survey of market participants and domestic regulations in numerous countries. Based on the results of the survey, the G10 emphasized market based governance and that countries should not expect bailouts the "size of Mexico".

Responsibility of the G7 and G8

Through these recent directives, the leaders demonstrated a recognition of the comparative advantages of the supranational organizations and the ability to construct well placed directives. They were not, however, timely nor were all directives fulfilled. There are a number of pressing issues that the G7 and G8 must address. (See Sachs, 1998, for a proposed agenda and a recommendation that the G8 be expanded to a G16.)

IMF Bailouts

Arguably most important is the problem of IMF bailouts. As is frequently argued, unlimited IMF bailouts increase the moral hazard of lending and borrowing activities.   Jeffrey Sachs (1998, p. 24) argues that the IMF worked "mightily and wrongheadedly" to make the world safe for "naive 25-year-old investment bankers who do not know much about world politics". Bailouts such as that in East Asia should cease.

Recent words of the G8 indicate that nations should not expect unlimited bailouts. It appears, however, that the IMF is continuing to approach problems as it has in the past and, thus IMF actions say otherwise. It is vital that the G7/G8 formulate a coherent and consistent approach to bailouts of future financial crises. The G7/G8 and the IMF must break the expectations they helped create. It is disappointing that the strongest statement the leaders could offer at the Birmingham summit was that "it is also important to ensure that the private sector plays a timely and appropriate role in crises resolution".[4]

IMF Responsibility

The G7 should shoulder the responsibility of actions being taken by the IMF. In contrast to organizations such as the United Nations, voting shares at the IMF are based on a weighted average as opposed to a "one nation, one vote" scheme. The weighted average voting power of the G7 increases for many important areas. On most issues, the G7 has 47% power and on the most important issues the G7's voting share is 70-80%. Hence, the G7 can define the broad agenda and block initiatives. In a 1998 testimony before the U.S. Congressional Joint Economic Committee, Paul Volcker (*Wall Street Journal*, 7 May 1998) stated that Congress "should pay less attention to the faceless bureaucrats at the IMF and focus more on where IMF policy on rescue packages really gets made. Your concerns should be addressed to Treasury".

IMF/World Bank Capabilities

In the longer-run, the G8 should rethink completely the role and even the necessity of the IMF and the World Bank. The G8 must first realize that the IMF is not technically equipped to deal with the types of financial crises that occur in the post-Bretton Woods era. Due to the increased integration of capital markets, the current crises have been fast-developing, financial in nature, and beyond the capacity of the Fund and other existing international organizations. As an example, the most current IMF Manual For Country Economists states:

A country will require IMF assistance when it is having balance of payments difficulties or, in other words, when the normal inflow of external savings is not sufficient to finance its resource gap, which is defined as the difference between domestic savings and domestic investment.

Next the G8 must realize that the current approach to Fund conditionality is counterproductive. Sachs (1998, p. 25), states that:

This process (conditionality) is out of hand. It has undermined political legitimacy in dozens of developing countries, especially since the IMF is often happy to conspire with governments to make end runs around parliaments in the interests of "reform". The contents of IMF programmes are too flawed to be a standard of good or poor performance. Markets realize this, so IMF programmes do less and less to rally them.

Supervisory Coordination

Finally, the G8 must further discussions on supervisory coordination. Primarily an initiative of Canadian Finance Minister Paul Martin, the issue should be expanded to include regulatory coordination in order to reduce regulatory arbitrage. In contrast to the Martin initiative, however, this should not lead to a new supranational body composed of governmental agents. It should be delegated to an agency with the greatest comparative advantage, perhaps the London Club or the Bank for International Settlements (BIS). It should also seek input from private sector practitioners as in today's financial environment, operational risk is greater the market risk. Bank management must therefore be involved.

Conclusion

It has been argued here that the G7, G8, and the summit process has failed to deal effectively with the most pressing economic issue of the day, that is, fast-developing liquidity crises of domestic financial sectors. The G7 and the G8 leaders have deferred these problems primarily to the IMF which has not the resources nor the technical ability to deal with such crises. Key agenda items should include the size and availability of bailout funds and the coordination of financial supervision and regulation. This is not an agenda for the new millennium. It is an agenda for today. At the turn of the millennium it may be much too late to address these issues.

Notes

1   According to one insider of the annual summits, the Japanese contingent brought up the impending financial problems in Thailand at the 1997 Denver summit. The other parties were uninterested and consequently the topic was dropped from discussions.

2   Soros, G. (15 September 1998), "The Crises of Global Capitalism", *The Wall Street Journal*, p. A22.

3   Soros, G. (15 September 1998), "The Crises of Global Capitalism", *The Wall Street Journal*, p. A22.

4   G8 Birmingham Summit Communiqué, 15-17 May 1998.

References

Caiola, M. (1995), *A Manual For Country Economists, Training Series Number 1, Volume 1,* International Monetary Fund.

Chang, R. and Velasco, A. (1998), "The Asian Liquidity Crisis", Federal Reserve Bank of Atlanta, Working Paper 98-11.

Daniels, J. P. and VanHoose D. D. (1999), *International Monetary and Financial Economics,* International Thompson Press / SouthWestern Publishing, Cincinnati.

Glick, R. (1998), "Capital Flows and Exchange Rates in the Pacific Basin", Federal Reserve Bank of San Francisco Economic Letter, #98-22.

Glick, R. and Rose, A. (1998), "How Do Currency Crises Spread?", Federal Reserve Bank of San Francisco Economic Letter, #98-25.

Goldstein, M. and Turner, P. (1996), "Banking Crises in Emerging Economies: Origins and Policy Options", *BIS Economic Papers,* No. 46.

Kenen, P. (ed) (1996), "From Halifax to Lyons: What Has Been Done about Crisis Management?", *Essays in International Finance,* #200, International Finance Section, Princeton University.

Lindgren, C., Gillian, G. and Saal, M. (1996), "Bank Soundness and Macroeconomic Policy", *International Monetary Fund*, Washington, D.C.

"Review and Outlook", (15 September 1998), *The Wall Street Journal,* pp. A22.

Sachs, J. (12 September 1998), "Global Capitalism: Making it Work", *The Economist,* pp. 23-25.

Soros, G. (15 September, 1998), "The Crises of Global Capitalism", *The Wall Street Journal,* pp. A22.

Von Hagen, J. and Fratianni, M. (1998), "Banking Regulation with Variable Geometry", in B. Eichengreen and J. Frieden (eds), *Forging an Integrated Europe,* The University of Michigan Press, pp. 159-184.

8 Promoting Growth in the World Economy

BRONWYN CURTIS (G-8)

For G1S
634

Introduction

What changes are desired to promote job growth and how are they to be achieved?[1] Specifically, how is Europe actually going to force these changes through?

Change is usually not undertaken voluntarily. It is necessity that forces change. If necessity can be linked with political or financial gain, the chances of change occurring are much higher. In regard to economic change, the driving forces for change are typically crisis and competition. The changes that are desirable are not always politically palatable. Often the impact of these changes are not felt until well into the next political cycle. Hence, the next government rather than the current one actually gains from them. What results is a short-term approach on the part of policymakers.

The Approach of the United States and the United Kingdom

Governments and the public everywhere would like to achieve what has recently been obtained in the United States. It is what those in the financial markets call the "Goldilocks Scenario". This consists of strong growth, low inflation, and low unemployment. Though there may be concerns about the distribution of gains between skilled labour and non-skilled labour, that is a question for separate consideration. The case for the approach taken by the United States in achieving the Goldilocks economy is proven. It is not, however, the only possible approach and may not be universally applicable.

Both the United Kingdom (UK) and United States have a boom and bust approach to economic growth. During the 1970s and 1980s the German Bundesbank was the only central bank that achieved price stability, and therefore a degree of economic stability. Amidst the two oil price crises of the 1970s and the beginning of the 1980s the Bundesbank earned its inflation-fighting credentials. As Figure 8.1 indicates, the U.S. Federal Reserve and the Bank of England were not nearly as successful. In the United States and in the United Kingdom there was much more volatility in the economic cycle.

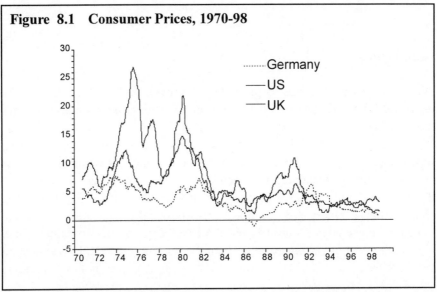

Figure 8.1   Consumer Prices, 1970-98

Source: Nomura International 1998

If there is a low degree of flexibility in the labour force, then during periods of volatility, an economy may move into real trouble. Labour force flexibility in the United States, and particularly in the United Kingdom, was forced through by economic necessity. Without this flexibility the economies could not adjust to the boom-and-bust cycles. One had to be able to have people coming into and leaving the labour force easily, otherwise the boom-and-bust cycle would be even more exaggerated. Hence, these two economies experienced changes in their degree of labour market flexibility. This process included undermining the strength of the unions.

The 1990s, however, is different from the earlier two decades. The 1990s have mostly enjoyed a more credible institutional framework. In this environment, expectations play a more important and key role in driving financial markets and economic policy. Thus, the credibility of economic policy has become critical.

Perception is perhaps more important than reality. The notion that independent central banks add credibility to economic policy and to the financial markets is very important. The United States achieved economic stability in the 1990s. To some extent, it is being reached in the United Kingdom, although it is not yet fully achieved. Nonetheless, as Figure 8.2 shows, following the Blair government's announcement of the Bank of England's independence, the differential between the yield on index-linked gilts and nominal gilts fell from about 4% to 3.5%. The yield differential can be considered a measure of the market's expectation regarding long-run inflation. This differential has continued to fall following the announcement as the British Government has shown its commitment to its inflation target.

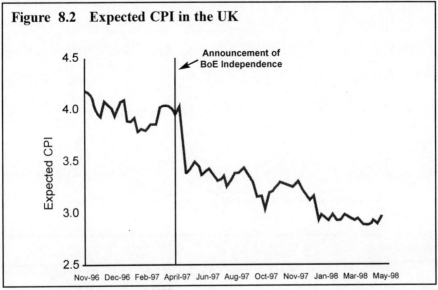

Figure 8.2 Expected CPI in the UK

Source: Nomura International 1998

Although it may be too early to conclude that this will be the outcome, the financial markets have already decided that central bank independence is a positive thing which will help achieve non-inflationary growth in the longer term. Arguably, then, the United States and the United Kingdom have achieved their Goldilocks economic results through flexibility in the labour market, followed by the implementation of sound monetary policy.

The European Approach

The German and European approach is quite different. Figure 8.3 shows that the average swings in the business cycles of Germany were much flatter than those of the United States for the 1972, 1978 and 1979/1985 cycles. There was less "boom and bust" in Germany than in the United States. Hence, there was less need for labour markets to be flexible, and less need for quick job creation and easy lay-offs.   Consequently, the economies of Europe could withstand higher costs of hiring and firing, higher overall taxation rates, and a larger social security system.

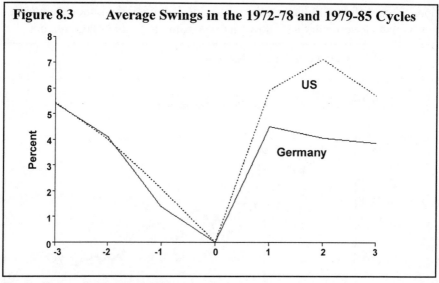

Figure 8.3   Average Swings in the 1972-78 and 1979-85 Cycles

Source: Nomura International 1998

The problem is that it is much harder to take away these high social safety nets once they are in place. Potential opponents argue that other countries should be attempting to bring their benefits up to one's own countries level. While it may be clear to politicians that reforms to the labour markets designed to foster employment and employability are important, they are unacceptable to most of the electorate. Who is going to vote for a politician who is advocating the equivalent of less job security and lower social security benefits whatever the overall benefit to the economy? Thus politicians are unlikely to initiate these changes unless they are forced to do so. The financial markets can force the issue.

The grim performance of the British economy during the 1970s and early 1980s provided an environment conducive to the reforms that Mrs. Thatcher brought about. In Italy, the collapse of the lira in 1992 and again in 1995, coupled with the threat of exclusion from the European Monetary Union (EMU) set the landscape for the privatisation of large state concerns, tighter fiscal policy, and the implementation of pension reforms. These policies would have been unthinkable in Italy if it were not for the serious crisis that it faced and the fact that it might not be included in EMU. This was the case in other countries as well. In Sweden it was the fear of default on their debt repayments which led to fiscal reform. This picture of crisis forcing change was also evident in Finland in the late 1980s and 1990s, when the loss of Russian trade forced the economy into recession and a major devaluation. This in turn led to a restructuring of the whole economy. Finland's finances are now in such good order that it has met the economic convergence criteria for EMU and will become a founding member. Subsequently, one can point to the restructuring taking place in the emerging economies of Southeast Asia.

None of these changes has taken place spontaneously. It has been forced upon countries by changes in the pricing of their assets in the financial markets. This is not a very happy state of affairs because the reforms are then usually very painful. They have to be undertaken in a difficult economic and financial environment. In every case, it was either economic/financial crisis or the expectation of it which forced through these changes. They were not undertaken willingly.

The other side of the argument is applicable to France and Germany in the late 1990s. It explains why virtually nothing has been done to reform the labour markets in these countries, despite an obvious need. These countries never had to fear that they would be excluded from EMU, because without them there would be no EMU. Although their economic performance in the 1990s has been disappointing, no crisis has resulted yet. Therefore it seems that some irretrievable deterioration in competitive position or crisis in France in Germany will be necessary to generate the labour market flexibility and mobility needed to cope with EMU. EMU will be the trigger which creates the necessary changes. Countries will not be able to just rely on market competition to achieve this, however as the legal framework of the labour market is tightly controlled and will have to be modified by each country.

Post EMU

The performance of the post-EMU European economies will be critical. As Figure 8.4 indicates, France and Germany represent about 55% of Gross Domestic Product (GDP) in the new "Euroland".[2] If one adds Italy, the figure rises to 75% of Euroland GDP. Thus, only 3 countries really matter in considering the post-EMU economy.

Figure 8.4   National Shares in Post-EMU Economy

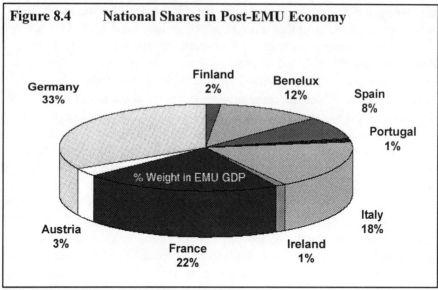

Source: Nomura International 1998

Monetary unification, however, is starting out at two speeds. As Figure 8.5 shows, the non-core Euroland countries such as Spain, Portugal and Ireland, are growing much more strongly than the core countries. The differences in economic performance means that the new single interest rate environment controlled by the European Central Bank (ECB) will be inappropriate for many of these countries. Six of the eleven countries forming Euroland (Italy, Spain, Portugal, Ireland, Finland and the Netherlands), which make up only one-third of Euroland GDP, need a higher or unchanged interest rate from what they have in mid-1998. The other five (Germany, France, Austria, Belgium and Luxemburg), which make up two-third of Euroland GDP, need stable rates or lower rates. Regardless of how policy is developed by the ECB, there will be a single interest rate and a single rate cannot suit everyone. As the ECB is governed on a one-country-one vote basis, rather than by a formula weighted by GDP share, the core countries will not be in control of interest rate policy. This could put Germany and France under pressure if interest rates are fixed higher than they can bear. In this environment, growth will be lower and unemployment, two-thirds of which is structural and rising with every economic cycle, will start expanding again.

The Growth and Stability Pact was established to ensure that countries like Italy, Spain, and Portugal kept budget deficits in line and pursued acceptable policies. The problem is that it will backfire as those countries,

Figure 8.5   European GDP Growth

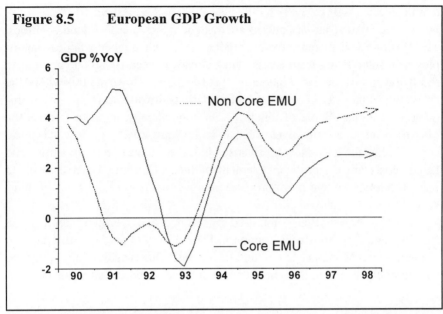

Source: Nomura International 1998

with the exception of Italy, are growing much more strongly than France and Germany. Furthermore, they will have lower interest rates and they will not have any problems in meeting their budget deficit targets. Even with higher interest rates these countries will have fewer problems meeting their budget deficit targets than the core countries will. These problems will intensify if high growth is not sustained at the start of EMU. Euroland is much more vulnerable to deceleration and deflation than the U.S. and the UK. Consumer confidence is quite fragile due to high levels of unemployment. As growth slows, unemployment will start to rise again and consumer confidence will be quickly undermined. Domestic multipliers aggravate the slowdown. France and Germany struggled to meet the budget deficit criteria of the Maastricht Treaty (3% or less of GDP) when growth was picking up. In this situation, where growth is already lower than in the rest of Europe, it is in France and Germany where public deficits will come under severe strain.

Assuming that the Euroland countries adhere to the rules of the Growth and Stability Pact, it will be this Pact which will force change. Even if the eleven Euroland members achieve the 2.6% growth per annum that they have achieved over the last 15 years, which is unlikely, Germany's budget deficit will rise well above 3% due to pension entitlements alone. The Organization for Economic Co-operation and Development (OECD) estimates that this deficit will be 3.6% by the year 2000 and a massive 16.1% of GDP by the year 2030. Similar patterns are evident in the other Euroland countries. The tensions will increase exponentially, as growth weakens, and as unemployment starts rising from levels which already exceed 10%. The immediate result may not be increased labour market flexibility. However, this will be the end result. One way of keeping budget deficits down is to privatise government institutions. Some of this has been done already, in order to meet the Maastricht criteria. However, there is still a long way to go to catch up to countries like the UK. Newly privatised industries have to be competitive and labour costs are a significant element of this. Catching up will result in increased lobbying and more pressure on governments to reform labour markets.

The Action Plan submitted by France and Germany for the G8 Employment Conference in London in February 1998 made no reference to Economic and Monetary Union and its impact. This is astounding, given the structural changes that this endeavour will force on European industry.

Structural Changes in Europe

It is important to consider these changes in industry and the service sector and therefore the changes in employment patterns in Europe, as restructuring forces the labour markets to be flexible. Even if the Growth and Stability Pact is ignored by the participants in Euroland, these other changes cannot be ignored. Once again, the biggest economies, France and Germany will bear the brunt of the industrial restructuring. Countries will face large real economy adjustments. If short term interest rates are more or less fixed, exchange rates fixed, and fiscal policy changes limited by the Pact, then the real economy and asset markets will bear the brunt of the adjustment. Not only will those adjustments to the real economy be larger, but competition will also force those changes through much faster than before.

Some might say that France and Germany will not adjust. After all, they have ignored the calls for change before. Their much more muted cycle meant that they did not need as much labour market flexibility as the U.S. and the UK. The countries entering Euroland have not yet achieved complete economic convergence, although more has been achieved than anyone thought possible in the early 1990s. However convergence is not complete. With EMU the adjustments to the real economies will be much greater than anything that those countries have encountered before. They will need to have much greater labour market flexibility than they have had in the past to cope with the scale of these economic changes.

Increases in Mergers and Acquisitions

In addition to the real economy adjustments for each country, the increased transparency will lead to behavioural changes by companies. A number of Euroland based companies have already developed a European-wide approach. However, there is much more to come. Large domestic companies see their market share being threatened, and believe that being bigger is the only way to survive. Organic growth is not going to be quick enough for many of companies with European or global aspirations. There has already been the merger between Daimler and Chrysler. This is just the tip of the iceberg. Merger and acquisition activity will increase once EMU is underway. This affects employment. Today's large domestic companies have the best chance of becoming the leaders in Europe. As these are mostly sited in the larger countries, the larger countries will become more, not less dominant.

During the current phase of "big is beautiful" driven by globalization, there are two processes underway. Regionally, within Euroland one will not need as many companies in many sectors because a few large companies can now operate across the whole bloc. Globally, if a firms wants to be a major force in the world in its area, and if this is an area where there is too much investment already, one probably needs to have global cross-alliances.

Financial Markets

There will also be considerable change in the financial sector. Europe is "over-banked". Most corporations now acquire about 60% of their funding through banks. This will change under monetary union, as it is much cheaper to fund through public markets. Over time the pattern of company funding in Europe will change and look more like that in the United States. In the United States most funding is through public markets, while only 20-30% of company funding is done through banks. The "big bets" on the pattern of restructuring are already being reflected in performances in the equity markets, both by country and sector (see Figure 8.6). In the real economy, sectoral changes like this take much longer to come to fruition. However, there is little doubt that they will occur. There are many more mergers ahead for the financial sector in Europe.

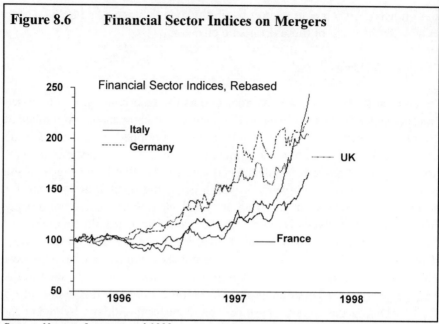

Figure 8.6   Financial Sector Indices on Mergers

Source: Nomura International 1998

Service Industries

Service industries will thrive in Euroland. Europe is already shifting away from manufacturing to services, just as in the United States and the United Kingdom. Monetary unification will prompt higher employment in service industries such as accounting, law, consultancy, travel, and leisure. The service sector in Europe, however, is very underdeveloped in many areas. Temporary employment is impossible. In contrast to others' assessments (Layard, 1999), it really is a big decision to employ someone in a country like Germany or France. Employment law is very heavily weighted towards the employee. Non-wage costs can undermine the financial viability of the whole venture. While this is not a bad thing in itself, it means that if it is possible to get the job done outside one of these countries, companies will do so. For some service industries this is not possible. However, others, like advertising, marketing and computing, which will be among the beneficiaries of the broader market, are easily carried out elsewhere. Retailing will become more competitive. Clearly, as Figure 8.7 shows, one will not drive from Denmark to Austria to buy a pair of Levi jeans. However when competition is applied to big products such as automobiles, competition will force change.

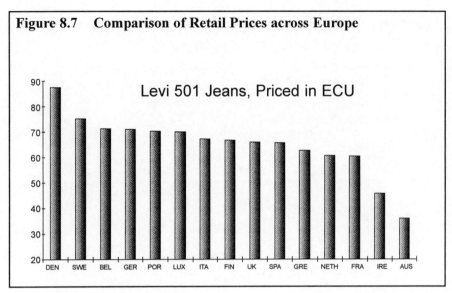

Figure 8.7   Comparison of Retail Prices across Europe

Source: Nomura International 1998

There is already one automobile company which is in the process of establishing a centralised sales operation.

Manufacturing

Low wage paying countries have received a strong boost to their manufacturing sectors in the second half of the 1990s. Investments will now spread to the east European countries where there will be more growth and more deregulated markets. In high cost countries, manufacturing will continue to decline as a percentage of GDP. Downward wage pressures are likely. These trends are already reflected in the equity markets. For example, the performance of the United Kingdom's manufacturing sector in the UK equity market is lagging behind that of the major European countries because the changes to this sector in the UK have already taken place. Hence, as Figure 8.8 indicates, the equity markets are suggesting that the potential for European manufacturing and service sectors is greater than those of the UK The UK has already reaped the rewards of the structural changes it forced in the 1980s. The potential future gains are much lower. Similar changes will take place with utilities, as there will be more privitisation of European utilities because of pressure on budget deficits (see Figure 8.9).

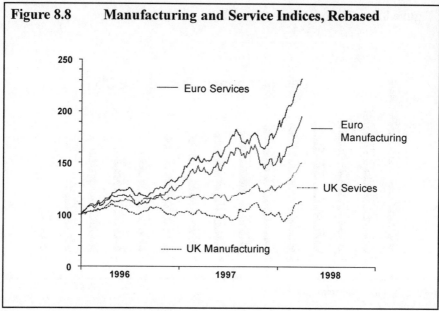

Figure 8.8   Manufacturing and Service Indices, Rebased

Source: Nomura International 1998

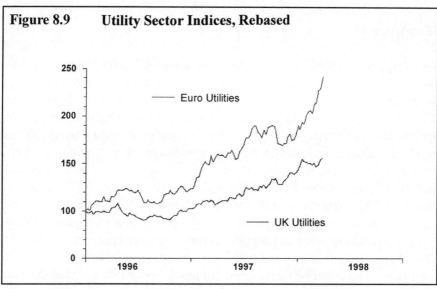

Figure 8.9   Utility Sector Indices, Rebased

Source: Nomura International 1998

Changes in Investment Patterns

The way in which people invest will change, as Table 8.1 shows. This will impact all of the various sectors. Continental fund managers and their clients have mostly invested thus far in bonds and a little bit of equity. This ratio will begin to reverse, particularly as governments will have to expand private pensions (see Figure 8.10). With more private pensions, investment will become more channeled into equities and less into bonds.

Table 8.1	Investment Fund Manager Portfolios			
Equities	**Bonds**	**Real**	**Other**	**Estate**
Germany	11	75	11	3
Switzerland	11	64	16	2
Netherlands	30	58	10	2
Denmark	22	65	9	4
Japan	29	63	3	5
USA	52	36	4	8
UK	80	11	6	3

Source: EFRP, UBS

Figure 8.10   Public Debt and Pension Liabilities as a Percentage of GDP

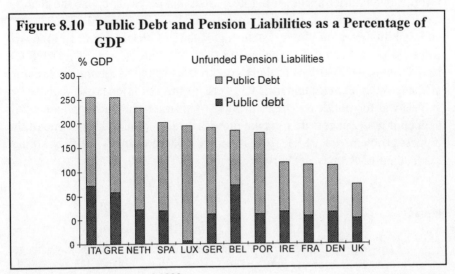

Source: Nomura International 1998

Conclusion

The structural reforms that are necessary in Euroland are quite clear. However they will never take place unless countries are forced by economic necessity to make these changes, for most of them are politically unpalatable. Although the end result may be the same, looking to the experiences of the U.S. and UK as a model is not the answer. Labour market reform was forced on the UK and U.S. because they were unable to control the "boom and bust" cycles in their economies. Here there was no choice but to have much more labour market flexibility to deal with these cycles. In contrast, Germany and France feel, quite rightly, that they have been able to develop and enjoy a much higher standard of social security and employment regulations than either the U.S. or UK because, until recently, their economic environment was more predictable and less volatile.

However, the problem has come to a head in the 1990s with the implementation of more credible economic policies in countries like the UK and the U.S. and the creation of their "Goldilocks" economies. In contrast, the price paid for the lack of flexibility in the face of upheavals in Europe with the reunification of Germany and the opening up of eastern Europe has been a higher level of unemployment in western Europe. So far, the Europeans have been able to pay for this. However, the added structural changes that EMU brings will force through changes in labour market reforms much faster than ever before. Crisis and necessity create the change. Change is not undertaken voluntarily, especially if it is painful. The Growth and Stability Pact and the restructuring of the industrial base in Europe will force major labour market changes in Germany and France. The 1998 G8 Employment Action Plans of these countries appeared to ignore the structural changes taking place under EMU. Perhaps this omission arose because the subject was too political to be confronted. This raises the question - what will happen if governments do not take these critical reforms? That is one of the biggest problems for EMU. EMU can force these changes. If they are not made, then EMU may not survive.

Notes

1   This chapter moves from Richard Layard's focus on the policy changes needed to promote job growth to how these policy changes can be achieved. It deals with Europe, where there has been much work on

deciding what is needed, but where very little has been achieved. Similar policy prescriptions can be applied elsewhere.

2   The term Euroland refers to the eleven members of the European Union who will be part of the European Monetary Union as of January 1, 1999. These are Germany, France, Italy, Spain, Ireland, the Netherlands, Luxemburg, Austria, Portugal, and Belgium.

Reference

Layard, R. (1999), "Designing Effective Policies for Employment Creation" in J. Daniels, M. Hodges and J. Kirton (eds.), *The G8's Role in the New Millennium*, Ashgate, Aldershot, pp. 159-167.

9 Managing the Global Economy

CHARLES GOODHART

(G-8) Fo2

Introduction

Discussions about possible reforms to the international financial architecture received considerable attention at the Birmingham Summit. This paper addresses some of the opportunities and consequences for policy actions, specifically in light of the 1997-98 East Asian financial crisis. However, this chapter is neither informed by, nor related to, my second role as a member of the Monetary Policy Committee (MPC) of the Bank of England and cannot be considered official policy.

The first section of this paper addresses the implications of the Asian crisis in regard to the appropriate exchange rate regimes that developing countries should adopt and maintain. The second section considers the need for improved financial regulation and how one might proceed towards that and the various issues on the appropriate sequencing of capital account liberalization. The third and fourth sections offer a reassessment of the International Monetary Fund's (IMF) response to what has been, and acknowledged as having been, essentially a private sector crisis, and the perennial request for yet more and better statistics. The final section provides a checklist of the winners and losers of the turmoil and disturbances of 1997-98.

The Appropriate Exchange Regime For Developing Countries

At a World Bank conference in Washington in 1998 James Tobin, used the opportunity to state that he thought there were increasingly strong arguments why countries, notably developing countries, should cease to adopt pegged but adjustable exchange rates. Once again such pegged notes have proven fragile to countries which adopted them, as in Thailand, Indonesia and Taiwan. Due to the crisis conditions, these countries were forced away from their currency peg and the resulting decline in their respective exchange rates proved too difficult to manage successfully. Floating exchange rate regime countries, such as Singapore, and the currency board arrangement of Hong Kong did rather better. It should be remembered, however, that their financial and exchange rate conditions were stronger to begin with.

One may also recall Steve Hanke's proposal that Indonesia should adopt a currency board arrangement. This proposal was severely criticized by the IMF. The IMF's position deserves the strongest support. Certain pre-conditions need to be in place if a country is going to adopt a currency board arrangement, or a similar situation with irrevocably fixed exchange rates. Those pre-conditions did not appear to be in place in Indonesia. Hence, the argument was made, and rightly so, that a currency board regime might, in due course, be appropriate in Indonesia, once it has strengthened its financial position and when appropriate changes to its political, economic and regulatory structure had been put in place. But this is not just yet.

Improved Financial Structure and Capital Account Liberalization

One of the main weaknesses that became apparent in several of these Asian countries, notably Thailand, Indonesia and Korea was the fragility of their banking systems, with numerous solvency problems. Undoubtedly more effective financial regulation and bank supervision would have been beneficial.

But the financial systems in these countries faced extreme price volatility in their asset markets, for example equities, property and, above all, their exchange rates. That would have been exceptionally testing even for the best regulated systems, as for example in Hong Kong. In particular, the exchange rate devaluations were not orderly and successful, but were more of an unstable rout.

One of the reasons for this was the reflux of previous short term capital inflows and the increasingly heavy weight of foreign currency denominated debt on the domestic borrowers. This naturally leads on to some reconsideration on whether completely free and open international capital markets should always be advocated. There are many proposals and suggestions being canvassed. One such was Chairman Greenspan's suggestion for some greater capital requirements to be introduced on net inter-bank positions. It is difficult, however, to envisage the complexities of introducing greater capital account requirements on net inter-bank positions worldwide. Indeed, it is difficult to imagine these requirements on inter-bank trading in individual financial centres such as London. There are surely now going to be some considerable delays in any further capital account liberalization until after the structure and regulation of domestic financial banking systems in developing countries have been much improved.

The IMF Response

There has been considerable criticism of the IMF, and reassessments are being undertaken of the Fund's response to the crisis. Normally in the post-war World War II years, a financial crisis resulted primarily from public sector laxity. This was not the case in the 19th century, however, and there are many aspects of what has happened in the East Asian crisis that are remarkably similar to this earlier period. The crises of the the 19th century affected countries such as Australia in 1893, the United States in 1907, and Italy in 1893, to name but a few.

Currently, the typical response of the IMF to the standard public sector crisis, caused by excessive public sector fiscal and monetary expansion, was to tighten fiscal policy, reduce subsidies, achieve better allocation via greater use of the market, raise interest rates and devalue the currency to a more sustainable level. But the countries involved in the recent crisis, notably Thailand, Indonesia, and Korea, were actually running, on average, fiscal surpluses before this crisis occurred. Further, the problem was not in the public sector. It was in the private sector, though it was indeed exacerbated by the exchange rate collapse impacting on the short-term net foreign currency indebtedness.

What is the appropriate response? The IMF continued to argue that there should be a certain degree of fiscal tightness and requested a continuation of fiscal surpluses despite the effect of automatic stabilizers that tend to drive the fiscal positions of these countries into deficit. These automatic stabilizers provide a degree of support for the domestic economy, notably the private sector economy.

To a large extent, the IMF has clearly relented and has moved back by lessening its requirements on these countries to run fiscal surpluses. Nonetheless, there is an argument in the IMF's favour that the bail-out of financial and banking systems will be be very expensive and will burden the taxpayer. Even if much of the short-term effect of the bail-out can be met by borrowing over the longer term, there will be a net annual annuity cost on the taxpayer in each of these countries arising from the bail-out itself.

This cost must be recognized.

Secondly, interest rate increases are undoubtedly necessary to provide some support for the foreign exchange market. But how much should the interest rate go up? For example, an interest rate of 10 percent or 15 percent, which would provide an interest differential over the United States of 10 percent or 1000 basis points, may be desirable. To go much further than that, however, may be an indication of panic and lead to such pressures on the domestic economy that it becomes counter-productive, as it is effectively a sign of weakness rather than strength.

It is difficult to choose the interest rate appropriate for these countries, because trying to choose how much is right, but not too much, is a matter of art which none can claim to be able to know with certainty. There is at least a case, however, that, even for external purposes, some of the interest rate increases as applied in Korea, for example, have been excessive and counterproductive rather than desirable and necessary.

Then there were the attempts to reduce subsidies, to improve the allocation properties of the market mechanism, to root out corruption, to open markets to competition, including foreign competition. But how far does such intervention become intervention in the sovereignty and appropriate domestic control of the affairs of the country involved. And what is to do be done about private sector indebtedness?

The IMF proved to be remarkably slow in trying to handle what was the crucial aspect of the whole crisis, the private sector indebtedness. The Fund also failed to get creditors and borrowers to come together and agree upon a sharing of costs. Undoubtedly there were going to be costs that had to be shared in terms of deferments and limitations on the amount of interest and principal that would and could be eventually paid back.

This raises the following question: Could there exist a trigger in borrowing covenants whereby, for example, if the IMF declares a country in crisis, automatically some of the fixed interest rate debt becomes, in part, a form of equity? Yet how would that be undertaken, if even possible? If it were to be undertaken, would the developed countries and the Group of Seven (G7) countries be prepared to put such clauses in their own bond covenants? If not, would the developing countries be prepared to do so?

The Importance of Statistics

One concern that arose is that in a couple of cases, at least, the statistics relating to a countries foreign exchange reserves were accurate but totally misleading. These data did not include the contingent claims arising from derivatives or from the possible hypothecation of the foreign exchange reserves to support commercial entities and commercial banks. There are now suggestions that foreign exchange reserves should be reported together with any contingency claims on them. One of the features of the crisis, as in the case of Korea, was that there were new data virtually every week in November about the extent of short term indebtedness. This is a grave problem, as how can one obtain data on short term indebtedness, either gross or net? Indeed, what is the short-term indebtedness, either gross or net, of the UK? It would be very difficult to obtain this information.

Winners and Losers

Finally, what are the effects of the recent East Asian crisis on of some of the players, and who are the winners and losers. Though this is entirely a subjective judgment, there is only one winner found in this exercise. This winner, however, is not a winner in an economic sense, but in the political sense. It is China.

China clearly is not a winner in the economic sense as its export markets have been reduced, though its export market is a relatively small proportion of its total economy. What happened in the case of China is that it was shown to be relatively strong despite the crisis. China is still growing relatively fast, indeed faster than any of the other neighbouring countries, and is seen to be an important and stable prop within the region. It is now clear, as it was not before this crisis, that Asia is not an area in which there is this v-shaped set of birds with Japan at the front. It is now a bipolar area with two giants in China and Japan. Further, with Japan weakening, the comparative strength of China has made it very clear that the comparative balance of political economic power within the Asian economies has shifted really quite dramatically in China's favour.

Moving to the United States, when the crises occurred, everybody wanted U.S. dollars. When the IMF went to the various countries, newspaper reports implied that there was usually somebody from the United States sitting in the anteroom, or even holding the IMF's hand. Undoubtedly the whole crisis has underlined the United States power and position. Yet given the checks and balances within the United States, for example the problems of the relationships between the executive and Congress, does the United States have the capacity to use that power in a quick and effective way and does it have the capacity to use that power in such a way as to make friends in East Asia? It is not at all clear whether the medicine that has been imposed on countries such as Korea has made the US appear to the inhabitants of those countries to be a more welcoming and friendly ally.

Among those that have been shaken but not really dislocated are the stronger Asian economies: Hong Kong, Singapore, Taiwan. The Philippines have come through better than might have been expected. One can add to this group the World Bank, since it has managed to avoid the criticisms that have rained down on the IMF.

Clearly weakened by the whole exercise have been the Fund, as described above, and Japan. Finally, dislocated and distressed have been South Korea, Thailand, Indonesia and Malaysia. How severe the outlook and how quickly they may bounce back from this particular difficulty surely will be the subject of differences of opinions. This will be answered over the course of the next two or three years.

Part III
The Broader Challenges

10 Negotiating Multilateral Rules to Promote Investment

ALAN RUGMAN

F02
F21
F23

(G-8, North America)

Introduction

One of the most important emerging economic and political issues for the Group of Seven/Group of Eight (G7/G8) leaders to address is the liberalization of investment. Today multinational enterprises (MNEs) dominate world trade and investment. Over half of the world's trade and over 80% of its foreign direct investment (FDI) is undertaken by MNEs based in the G7 countries, namely the United States, Japan, Canada and the large countries of Western Europe (Rugman, 1996; United Nations, 1997). While tariffs and many non-tariff barriers to trade have been negotiated away in seven successive rounds of the General Agreement on Tariffs and Trade (GATT), the issue of investment liberalization has been largely ignored. Only in the North American Free Trade Agreement (NAFTA) has investment been a central part of a trade agreement. The investment provision of NAFTA have been seen as a model for a multilateral agreement on investment (MAI).[1]

An important topic for the 1998 Birmingham summit and subsequent summits of the G7/G8 should be how to rescue the MAI from imminent failure. The design and adoption of a clear set of multilateral investment rules should be a priority for the G7/G8 leaders. This chapter first discusses the reasons for the political failure of the MAI, despite its economic benefits. It then uses the Canadian experience with the MAI to illustrate the negative side of the involvement of non-governmental organizations (NGOs) in the MAI process.

This chapter explains the relationship of the MAI to NAFTA, the nature of opposition to the MAI by Canadian-based NGOs, and the nature and content of the MAI. It considers the difference between shallow and deep integration, the role of MNEs, and the impact of the MAI on Canada. This impact is found to be neutral, since NAFTA already provides the major benefit of the MAI, through opening up investment with the United States.

The Political Failure of the MAI

The life of the MAI can be benchmarked from the Halifax G7 summit of 1995 to the G8 Birmingham summit of 1998.[2] At the Halifax summit, in June 1995, the final G7 communiqué endorsed the negotiation of a set of multilateral rules for investment at the Paris-based Organization for Economic Cooperation and Development (OECD). Almost concurrently, ministers and delegates at the OECD launched technical and substantive discussions, hoping to conclude the MAI within two years, by April 1997.[3] Failure to conclude the negotiations at that date led to a one-year extension. However, by April 1998 it was clear that final agreement on the MAI was still far off, so a pause in negotiations of six months was accepted. Without a deadline to force agreement, such a pause (which can lead into an indefinite delay) signals the political failure of the MAI.

In time, the substantive issues of the MAI may be taken up at the Geneva-based World Trade Organisation (WTO), but probably only as part of a new round of multilateral trade negotiations. The last, Uruguay Round, of the GATT took seven years to complete, so the immediate prospects for negotiating a MAI, at the WTO, are not good. It will be even more difficult to generate a consensus, as there are 132 members of the WTO, as opposed to only 29 members of the OECD. About 90% of all the world's stock of FDI is held by the 29 OECD members, which are rich developed countries from Western Europe, North America and Asia. The economic logic of the OECD as the forum for discussion of rules for FDI remains strong, even if the political logic of formal involvement of all parties (including developing countries) through the WTO is of increasing relevance. However, it has become obvious that the real reason for the defeat of the MAI has less to do with whether the OECD or WTO is the better forum, and more to do with the negative role of NGOs as critics of international trade agreements.

The Power of NGOs

The NGOs are a new and powerful actor on the stage of international business. In the 1997 to 1998 period, NGOs assumed a more effective role than previously observed, leading to the defeat of the MAI at the OECD. Prominent in orchestrating the NGOs was Canada's self-promoting Council of Canadians, chaired by economic nationalist Maude Barlow. In a clever campaign of misinformation and half-truths, exhibited in the Clarke and

Barlow booklet on the MAI (Clarke and Barlow, 1997), the Council filled the web sites of various NGOs with anti-MAI hysteria that proved influential with the media.

With the U.S. and Canadian governments treating the MAI on a technical rather than political level and with ministers being poorly briefed by their trade officials, there was little political will to counter the gross distortion of the MAI offered by unelected and unaccountable NGOs. In addition, business leaders were unwilling to speak out on the advantages of the MAI, leaving the defense of the MAI to a handful of industry association spokespeople. Finally, the academic world (with a few exceptions) had not researched the issue. This was especially true of economists who have no theory parallel to free trade to apply to the liberalization of investment. Consequently almost none were available or willing to publicly debate the substantive issues of the MAI while engaged in their full-time professional duties. The absence of informed government, business and academic commentary left the media open to the distorted propaganda of unrepresentative NGOs.

The success of the NGOs in defeating the MAI builds upon their less spectacular but consistent progress in capturing the environmental agenda of international organizations. The first notable success of environmental NGOs (entirely U.S. and Canadian) occurred in NAFTA when the first Clinton administration in 1993 inserted two side agreements after NAFTA had been successfully negotiated by the Bush administration in the 1990-1992 period. These side agreements established an environmental body, the Commission for Environmental Cooperation (CEC) in Montreal and a labour standards body, the Commission for Labour Cooperation (CLC) in Dallas.[4]

The United Nations Conference on Environment and Development (UNCED), or Rio Summit, was a jamboree for environmental NGOs, leading to an unbalanced agreement with sets of commitments which the governments were unable to deliver. Despite these lessons, the follow-on Kyoto Summit in December 1997 resulted in standards for reduction of greenhouse gas emissions that, again, most countries will not themselves meet. Indeed, ratification of the Kyoto protocol is unlikely, as only the EU appears to have the political will to ratify it, whereas the United States, Canada, Japan and many other countries are highly unlikely to do so. In Canada's case this is due to the federal nature of the country, where the provinces have the power to control natural resources. Thus, Alberta as the largest energy producing province, will need to agree to implement Kyoto in order for the Government of Canada to accept its obligations under the treaty.

The Role of NGOs in the MAI

These recent events portray a gulf between the environmental agendas of the NGOs and the economic reality of global business. To explain this dichotomy, two theories are useful. First, there is a traditional divide between the redistributional/equity concerns of NGOs and the economic/efficiency drivers of business. Democratic governments in Western economies have been able to balance these dual concerns when they embed different weights to these goals in their political platforms, giving voters the ultimate voice in the direction to be followed. Recently, this formula has not worked, as NGOs are operating outside of democratic political representation.

For example, having failed to influence the Liberal Party of Canada, (now the Canadian government) Maude Barlow has chaired the Council of Canadians as it performs as a self-standing political unit. In the 1993 federal election the Council supported the economic nationalist party led by Edmonton publisher Mel Hurtig. In that election, despite fielding a national slate of candidates, Hurtig's party secured less than 1% of the total popular vote. Yet, this complete rejection of the economic nationalist platform of Hurtig and the Council of Canadians (including its opposition to NAFTA) was completely ignored by Maude Barlow's Council of Canadians. It has continued with a nationalist agenda even though this stance is divorced from the party platforms of all of Canada's major political parties. A similar non-representative and politically unacceptable behavior is undertaken by most U.S. and European NGOs. Whereas the labour movement and business groups are linked directly to political parties and have their agendas directly voted upon in elections, most NGOs are afraid to face the voters. Yet their unrepresentative views gain vastly disproportionate influence in the media.

The second factor is complementary to the undemocratic nature of NGOs, particularly in their biased understanding of international trade and investment. This is an intellectual failure of academic theory in which the twin basic paradigms of economics and politics are found wanting as explanations of today's global economy and the nature of FDI. In economics, the traditional efficiency-based neoclassical paradigm, with its associated theory of comparative advantage and the overall country gains from free trade, is unsuitable as an explanation of FDI. Despite the efforts by international business scholars over the last 30 years to develop a modern theory of the multinational enterprise, most economists are unable to accept their explanation of the reasons for FDI (Rugman, 1996). As a consequence, the GATT and WTO have developed institutional frameworks to deal with the "shallow" integration of tariff cuts, but have failed to deal with the "deep" integration of FDI.

Related to the out-of-date economics paradigm of free trade is the political science focus on the nation state. Despite minor modifications to nation state paradigms, for example, by incorporating sub-national units in decision making, there remains a limited acceptance of the alternative International Political Economy (IPE) viewpoint first popularized by Susan Strange in 1987. Indeed, there is another unfortunate parallel between economics and political science in that both sets of work on the role and power of the MNE have failed to change the obsolete thinking of the majority of academics. This comes despite the abundant evidence of the relevance of MNEs to the global economic and political systems of today. Into this vacuum the NGOs have slipped with their simplistic view of MNEs as big, bad and ugly. Based on prejudice rather than evidence, the NGO thinking is now more influential with governments in North America and Europe than is the more scientific (and thereby more qualified) work of serious scholars working on MNEs (Ostry, 1997).

The issue here is one of process. There is an "administrative heritage" of ideas. Today's media are poorly trained in economics, politics and international business. Those few who have any training are usually victims of the dated paradigms of traditional economics and political science which cannot explain FDI and the MNEs. The MBAs of business schools, who are now exposed to the new thinking on MNEs, are in business rather than the media. The professional intermediaries, such as management consultants, are focused on their business or government clients rather than the media. Moreover, their very skills of confidential advice and in-house retraining make them poor advocates in comparison to the pessimistic and opinionated NGOs. Finally, the civil service has failed in publicly dealing with NGOs as officials attempt to support and influence ministers rather than entering into the public forum. This institutional failure on the part of academics, consultants and officials to prepare a credible case for the MAI and their inability to publicly debate its merits leaves the field open to NGOs.

Although the NGOs can be partly credited with the defeat of the MAI, the primary reason lies elsewhere. Even with the high profile activities of NGOs in 1997 and 1998, the MAI would likely still have been concluded at the OECD if the United States had been properly organized. The right of the U.S. Congress to pass trade laws and the corresponding current lack of power by the President to negotiate international trade and investment treaties is the real explanation for the delay of the MAI. The failure by President Clinton to obtain "fast track" negotiating authority from Congress in autumn 1997 (for a free trade area of the Americas, but also for a future round of the WTO, and for an MAI) was the single most important reason for the failure of the MAI. The NGOs were able to slip into this vacuum and steal the agenda.

Without the full commitment of the United States to champion a trade or investment agreement, there is little hope of success for the MAI process. All countries will face lobbying by various producer groups to exempt certain sectors from national treatment (for example, cultural industries for Canada and France). To broker an international agreement the full participation of the United States is vital, as it is still the only country powerful enough to pull along other countries rife with internal dissent and sectional interests. Yet while President Clinton pushed through NAFTA in 1993, he has been unable to assemble a coalition to follow any free trade and investment liberalization initiatives since.

Canada and the MAI

During the Canadian federal election campaign in May 1997, the Council of Canadians and various other left-wing NGOs, such as the Canadian Labour Congress, the Sierra Club of Canada and Citizens Concerned About Free Trade, ran full page newspaper advertisments criticizing the MAI. At the time the MAI was still being negotiated in Paris at the OECD. May 1998 was the extended completion date. But even as this date approached, discussion was postponed for several months.

Maude Barlow's Council of Canadians states that "the new MAI gives transnational corporations (TNCs) so much power that Parliament won't matter". More specific statements include the allegations that the MAI "cripples Canada's ability to create jobs", "paves the way for a two-tiered health system", "guts our ability to protect our environment", and "leaves Canada's culture at the mercy of U.S. entertainment mega-corporations".

None of these statements is accurate. They convey a misleading picture that alleges that the MAI will introduce changes adversely affecting Canadian sovereignty and economic control. In reality, the MAI will not bring any significant economic or political changes to Canada since Canada already has a de facto MAI with the United States - in the Canada-US Free Trade Agreement (FTA) of 1989.

The investment provisions of the FTA that took effect on January 1, 1989, are the basis of the draft MAI. The NAFTA investment provisions of 1993 were based upon the FTA. These NAFTA investment provisions are identical in all major respects to those in the draft MAI. For example, both the FTA and NAFTA incorporate the key principle of national treatment, i.e. equal access for foreign (U.S.) investors to the Canadian market but according to Canadian rules. In return, Canadian investors have equal access to foreign (U.S.) markets, on host country rules. Both the FTA and NAFTA also have exemptions from national treatment for important Canadian sectors, including the "big five" of health care, education, social services, cultural industries and transportation.

The MAI is being negotiated along similar lines. Countries have agreed to the principle of national treatment but they disagree over the number and type of exempted sectors. It is clear that the Canadian government will continue to insist on exemptions for the five sectors, especially culture, and that the logic of the FTA/NAFTA will be used as a model for the MAI. The underlying structure of the FTA, NAFTA and MAI is now well understood by Canadians as a clever balance between the pressures of globalization (national treatment) and the need for national sovereignty (exempted sectors).

The current challenge in international trade negotiations, somewhat paradoxically, is to negotiate investment rules rather than trade rules. This is because, as a result of seven GATT rounds and important bilateral agreements such as the FTA, the best known barriers to trade, in the form of tariffs, have already been reduced to a trivial hurdle. This is so even when calculating effective rates of protection (which take into account the value added and labour component of the protected good.)

Today, the majority of international business does not take the form of trade in goods, but operates through trade in services and investments. Over 70% of North Americans work in the service sector, with only 30% in manufacturing. As a consequence, the new agenda for international agreements is to negotiate rules for trade in services and for international investment (Ostry, 1997). The "shallow" integration achieved by reducing tariff barriers to trade in goods is being replaced by "deep" integration through FDI, trade in services and the international networks of multinational enterprises (Brewer and Young, 1998).

The MAI at the OECD

The structure of the MAI follows that of NAFTA. It is built upon a platform with four central elements. The first is the principle of national treatment with lists of exempted sectors. The second is transparency, the principle that all regulations on investment are identified as are all exemptions to the principle of national treatment. The third is a dispute settlement mechanism, to permit individual investors (and companies) to appeal against government regulations and bureaucratic controls. The fourth is a movement towards the harmonization of regulations, although in the areas of competition policy and tax policy not much progress can be expected in the MAI (and none was achieved in NAFTA).

In the draft MAI all of these four areas have been addressed. The structure of the MAI is based upon NAFTA's investment provisions, as was predictable. The aim of the MAI is to make domestic markets internationally contestable by providing a basic set of rules for FDI to which all member countries agree. The OECD in Paris is the correct venue to negotiate the MAI as 98% of all the world's FDI is conducted by MNEs based in the 29 member countries of the OECD, such as those in all of Western Europe, North America, Japan, Korea, Australia and New Zealand. There is some opposition to the MAI in a few of the poorer developing countries. However, until the WTO begins to move on investment issues, there is no practical alternative to the OECD as a venue for the MAI.

Another reason for the MAI being negotiated at the OECD is that it builds upon several existing OECD investment instruments, including a code of conduct for MNEs from 1975 (Safarian, 1993). The OECD has been the group working for the last quarter century to establish a binding set of legal rules for foreign investment and ensure market access for investment according to the principle of national treatment. Expert opinion has agreed that developing countries would benefit from an MAI as it would encourage long-term investment and support sustainable development (Fitzgerald, 1998). Such studies did not support the concern that developing countries would lose economic sovereignty due to an MAI. Nor was there any question of an MAI leading to lower environmental and labour standards, as argued by NGOs.

The MAI and NAFTA

The draft MAI is similar to the NAFTA investment regime in all substantive respects and in most procedural detail. The critics of the MAI have misunderstood the technical details of the MAI (as they did the FTA and NAFTA). For example, opponents claim that there are tighter mechanisms for "standstill" and "rollback". Here, "standstill" means that countries cannot impose any new regulations to restrict investment; while "rollback" means that countries agree to a timetable to reduce existing regulations on investment. These are technical and legal terms intended to make the MAI function effectively. These process-related issues do not add to the economic or political substance of the MAI in any way when compared to NAFTA. There are similar provisions in NAFTA. There is, in fact, a large overlap in the technical and legal procedures of the proposed MAI and the existing NAFTA. In turn, there was a very strong overlap between the investment provisions of NAFTA and those of the earlier FTA.

One issue seized upon by NGOs is the first NAFTA-based investor-state appeal case brought by U.S.-owned Ethyl Corporation. They are the sole manufacturers in Canada of a gasoline additive, MMT, which was banned by the Canadian government in 1997. Although this is the first case in the first four years of NAFTA that has been taken into a Chapter 11 dispute settlement process, NGOs use it as an example to criticize the MAI (Rugman, Kirton and Soloway, 1999). They generalize the specifics of this case to claim that foreign investors could use the expropriation provision of an MAI to claim compensation for loss of business when an environmental regulation is passed. They argue that any harm on any foreign-owned property or product would qualify for MAI protection.

All of this is misconceived. All an MAI can do is apply the principle of national treatment. Environment regulations can still be adopted by countries, before or after an MAI, without the MAI making any difference. All that the MAI can require is that foreign-owned firms are treated in the same way as domestic firms in the face of new legislation. The issue of there being a monopoly foreign supplier is a different issue, better handled by economic-based competition policy than by any aspect of the MAI. Of course, there exists the possibility that lawyers will improperly apply the MAI as it will produce a set of multilateral investment laws. The issue of eminent domain (the power of a sovereign country to regulate) and the law of "taking" is a matter for legal interpretations, which can differ between regimes. However, the MAI cannot confer more power in law on a foreign-owned firm. All the MAI can do is make a foreign firm equal to a domestic firm in law.

The Economic Logic of the MAI

While the intellectual foundations of the MAI are to be found in the FTA of 1989, the economic and political dynamics of the MAI are also based on the

FTA. In terms of inward and outward FDI, 70% of Canada's total is with the United States. This very large share is already governed by the rules inherent in the FTA and NAFTA. Therefore, the MAI will not bring any changes to investment rules for the great majority of Canada's FDI. As a result, the MAI cannot create any major new pressures on jobs, health or culture. As for the environment, the NAFTA was the first international trade and investment agreement to explicitly consider the environment, both in its core text and through a side agreement. There now exists a NAFTA-based CEC which is beginning to research, assess and help improve cooperation on environmental issues in Mexico as well as in Canada and the United States. While in the draft MAI there are no similar environmental provisions, Canada retains the benefits of NAFTA's environmental measures for over 70% of its trade and investment linkages.

The long-term, underlying logic of the FTA, NAFTA and MAI from a Canadian perspective is driven by the extraordinarily high level of integration of the Canadian and U.S. economic systems. As is well known, for the 20 years prior to 1998 over two thirds of Canada's trade has been with the United States. Indeed, Canadian exports to the United States have increased from 64% in 1981 to 73% in 1987 (at the time of the FTA) and again to 82% by 1996. Perhaps less well known is that while Canada's inward FDI follows a similar course (in 1996, 68% of the stock of all inward FDI was from the United States), Canada's outward FDI has become much more diversified. In 1996, only 54% of all Canadian outward FDI stock could be found in the United States. There had been as much as 66% of Canada's outward FDI stock in the United States in 1987 but during the 1990s it diversified to the EU (now 20%) and Asia (although there is still only 1.6% in Japan). While these data still confirm the tremendous economic interdependence of Canada and the United States, they explain why the MAI will be of benefit to Canadian business as it continues to diversify to Europe and Asia.

The MAI is a good news story. The other side of the national treatment coin is that Canadian outward FDI will be encouraged by an MAI. Indeed, as a non-member of the triad (the United States, European Union and Japan) Canada is a small, open economy dependent on access to triad markets. Today this access is more often achieved through FDI than through trade (although FDI and trade are highly positively correlated). While 54% of Canada FDI stock is in the United States (and thereby already has national treatment) the MAI will be very useful in setting stable rules for the rapidly increasing stock of Canadian FDI outside the U.S., especially in the EU and Asia. The MAI should thus help Canada to continue to diversify its outward

FDI away from the United States. Of particular relevance in the MAI will be investment rules to ensure Canadian business has stable access to the EU in resource-based sectors such as forestry products, where there has been a wave of protectionism during the 1990s. The MAI should also help to open up the Japanese, other Asian and Latin American markets for Canadian FDI.

While the MAI can help reduce Canada's economic dependence on the United States, it is important to keep in mind the regional nature of business in North America. Table 10.1 reports the bilateral stocks of FDI between Canada and the United States over the twenty years to 1996. The most striking point is that over this period there has been a dramatic increase in the relative amount of Canadian outward FDI to the United States compared to U.S. FDI in Canada. The last column of Table 1 shows that in 1976 the ratio of outward Canadian FDI in the United States to inward U.S. in Canada was only 20%. Thus there was five times as much U.S. FDI in Canada as Canadian FDI in the United States. Even in 1976 this was good news, since Canada was only one tenth the size of the U.S. economy, but had twice as much FDI in the United States as would have been expected on the basis of relative size. By 1985 the ratio of bilateral Canadian outward FDI to inward FDI had tripled to 62%. At the time the FTA was being negotiated in 1987 it was 66%. In the ten years since the FTA took effect, the ratio continued to increase. In 1996 it stood at 76%.

Behind these figures lies the untold story of the success of the FTA. Canadian-based MNEs are doing well in the U.S. market. They have developed as viable parts of business networks and economic clusters on a North American regional basis. Today there is no such thing as a Canadian business - they are all North American businesses. Although Canada remains one tenth the size of the U.S. economy, Canada has access to the U.S. market via FDI, to the extent that the ratio of bilateral outward to inward FDI is 76%, or at least seven times larger than is expected by relative size alone. The MAI will provide stable rules to help Canadian business experience the same sort of market access in Europe and Asia.

The Canadian-owned MNEs that are doing well in the highly competitive, global U.S. market include Nortel, Alcan, Noranda, Moore, International Thompson, Bombardier, and Bank of Montreal. In addition, the U.S. MNEs in Canada, such as G.M., Ford, Chrysler, IBM and DuPont, contribute to Canada's economy by providing jobs and paying taxes. Together the 50 largest Canadian-owned MNEs in the United States and U.S.-owned MNEs in Canada account for 90% of all two way FDI and well over 70% of all bilateral trade. The three U.S.-owned auto assemblers themselves lead a

Table 10.1 FDI Between Canada and the U.S., 1980-96

A Year	B Canadian FDI in the U.S. (Cdn. $m)	C U.S. FDI in Canada (Cdn. $m)	D (B) (C)*
1976	6,547	32,726	20.0
1977	7,651	35,595	21.5
1978	9,615	39,352	24.4
1979	12,976	44,006	29.5
1980	17,849	50,386	35.4
1981	23,695	53,777	44.1
1982	25,189	54,457	46.3
1983	30,262	59,706	50.7
1984	36,683	64,762	56.6
1985	41,851	67,874	61.7
1986	44,461	69,241	64.2
1987	48,876	74,022	66.0
1988	51,025	76,049	67.1
1989	56,578	80,427	70.3
1990	60,049	84,089	71.4
1991	63,379	86,396	73.4
1992	64,502	88,161	73.2
1993	67,770	90,477	74.9
1994	76,781	102,035	75.2
1995	86,466	112,485	76.9
1996	92,907	122,722	75.7
Average rate of increase	14.6	6.9	

Source: Statistics Canada, Canada's International Investment Position,Catalogue 67-202, 1926-1996

cluster that accounts for one third of all U.S.-Canadian trade. These features were known during the FTA negotiations in 1985-1987. The story of North America economic integration is reflected in the FTA and NAFTA, and now in the MAI.

One of the exemptions in the MAI is for national security. This is a loophole inserted by the United States to allow it to subsidize high tech consortia and continue current discriminatory practices against the U.S. subsidiaries of foreign MNEs. This is a type of "conditional" national treatment affecting research and development. It is one that the NAFTA also permits. It remains one of the areas where misguided advocates of national competitiveness and strategic trade policy pin their hopes for an industrial/science policy.

It is to prevent such discriminatory measures by triad members that the MAI is designed. It is in the economic interests of smaller countries like Canada to criticize the conditional national treatment of others and to refrain from using it themselves. The latter is a simple choice since a national indus-trial/science policy for Canada is doomed to economic failure, as it protects small market Canadian-based businesses and discourages more useful inward FDI. More importantly, the MAI is highly unlikely to change current NAFTA-based practice permitting research and development and condition-al national treatment. Thus Canada is not much affected by the MAI in the area of science and technology.

Conclusions

In general, because investment has a long-term time horizon, business peo-ple need to be assured that political risk is low. New and capricious invest-ment regulations deter FDI and thereby reduce global economic efficiency. Canada has mitigated the worst excesses of left wing economic nationalism through the investment provisions of the FTA and NAFTA. The MAI is the icing on the cake of globalization for Canada.

Once again, the MAI is a good news story. All of the substantive concerns raised by the Council of Canadians were first dealt with in the 1980s in the satisfactory negotiations for the FTA. These answers were reaf-firmed in NAFTA. The NAFTA is such an advanced trade and investment pact that it is being used as the model for the MAI. Given that Canada has survived quite well during the first decade of the investment provisions of the FTA, it is well placed to accept the MAI. The MAI has the additional advan-tage of helping to open up markets in Europe and Asia for Canadian investors on the same terms as in the U.S. market.

Notes

1   The MAI is reviewed in this chapter from the perspective of an academic Canadian commentator now relocated to England. For further discussion of the relationship between NAFTA and the MAI and the argument that the MAI could be based on the investment provisions of NAFTA, see Gestrin and Rugman (1996), Rugman and Gestrin (1996) and Rugman (1997). For discussion of the investment process of NAFTA see Rugman (1994).

2   At a pre-summit conference in Halifax in May 1995, several academic papers expressed the need for an MAI. These included those subsequently published by Rugman and D'Cruz (1997) and by Winham and Grant (1997). Other contributions include Brewer & Young (1995) and Smith (1995).

3   In mid-1994 the OECD organised a conference on trade, investment, competition and technology policies to develop a "New Trade Agenda" with more of a focus on the issues of "deep integration" (ie. investment related) rather than the traditional "shallow integration" of tariff cuts. Following this, the OECD organised a series of Trade Committee sessions at which several important papers were prepared which laid out a policy for the MAI. The most important of these were subsequently published by Gestrin & Rugman (1996), Lawrence (1996), and Graham (1996).

4   For discussion of the political process in the United States at the time of approval of NAFTA see Susan Liebler in Rugman (1994).

References

Brewer, T. L. and Young, S. (1995), "The Multilateral Agenda for Foreign Direct Investment: Problems, Principles and Priorities for Negotiation at the OECD and WTO", *World Competition* 18(4), 67-83.

Brewer, T. L. and Young, S. (1998), *Multilateral Investment Rules and Multinational Enterprises,* Oxford University Press, Oxford.

Clarke, T. and Barlow, M. (1997), *MAI: The Multilateral Agreement on Investment and the Threat to Canadian Sovereignty,* Stoddart, Toronto.

Fitzgerald, E. V. K. (1998), "The Development Implications of the Multilateral Agreement on Investment", an independent study for the Department for International Development of the United Kingdom, Queen Elizabeth House, Oxford.

Gestrin, M. and Rugman, A. M. (1996), "The NAFTA Investment provisions: Prototype for Multinational Investment Rules" in P. Sauvé and A. B. Zampetti (eds.), *Market Access after the Uruguay Round: Investment, Competition and Technology Perspectives,* OECD, Paris, pp.63-78.

Graham, E. M. (1996), "Investment and the New Multilateral Trade Context", in P. Sauvé and A. B. Zampetti (eds.), *Market Access after the Uruguay Round: Investment, Competition and Technology Perspectives,* OECD, Paris, pp.35-62.

Lawrence, R. Z. (1996), "Towards Globally Contestable Markets", in P. Sauvé and A. B. Zampetti (eds.), *Market Access after the Uruguay Round: Investment, Competition and Technology Perspectives,* OECD, Paris, pp.25-34.

Ostry, S. (1997), *The Post-Cold War Trading System: Who's on First?,* University of Chicago Press, Chicago.

Rugman, A. M. (1994), (ed.) *Foreign Investment and NAFTA,* University of South Carolina Press, Columbia, S.C.

Rugman, A. M. (1996), *Multinational Enterprises and Trade Policy,* Elgar, Cheltenham.

Rugman, A. M. (1997), "New Rules for Multinational Investment", *The International Executive* 39(1), pp. 21-33.

Rugman, A. M. and D'Cruz, J. (1997a), "Strategies of Multinational Enterprises and Governments: The Theory of The Flagship Firm", in G. Boyd and A. M. Rugman (eds.), *Euro-Pacific Investment and Trade: Strategies and Structural Interdependencies,* Elgar, Cheltenham, pp.37-68.

Rugman, A. M. and Gestrin, M. (1996), "A Conceptual Framework for a Multilateral Agreement in Investment: Learning from the NAFTA", in P. Sauvé and D. Schwanen (eds.), *Investment Rules for the Global Economy,* C.D. Howe Institute, Toronto, pp.147-175.

Rugman, A., Kirton, J. and Soloway, J. (1999), *Environmental Regulations and Corporate Strategy: A NAFTA Perspective,* Oxford University Press, Oxford.

Safarian, A. E. (1993), *Multinational Enterprises and Public Policy,* Elgar, Cheltenham.

Smith, A. (1995), "The Development of a Multilateral Agreement on Investment at the OECD: A Preview", in C. J. Green and T. L. Brewer (eds.) *Investment Issues in Asia and the Pacific Rim,* Oceana, Dobbs Ferry, New York, pp.101-112.

Strange, S. (1987), *States are Markets: An Introduction to International Political Economy,* Pinter, London.

United Nations (1997), *World Investment Report 1997,* UNCTAD, Geneva.

Winham, G. and Grant, H. A. (1997), "Designing Institutions for Global Economic Co-operation: Investment and the WTO", Paper for Halifax Pre-G7 Summit Conference, May 1995, in G. Boyd and A. M. Rugman, (eds.), *Euro-Pacific Investment and Trade: Strategies and Structural Interdependencies,* Edward Elgar, Brookfield, VT., pp.248-272.

11 Designing Effective Policies for Employment Creation

RICHARD LAYARD

E24   (G-8)
Fo2
F16 F41

Introduction

It is highly appropriate that employment was one of the major themes at the Birmingham Summit. Considering western society, especially the society in continental Europe, the most scandalous failure is on the employment front. People need an income and they also need to be needed. If you are of working age, the way to satisfy both these needs is through a job. A society which accepts mass unemployment, mitigated by hand-outs, will leave millions with empty lives.

This chapter discusses the possible causes of high European unemployment and the solutions which would be implied by those causes. The six most common solutions that are suggested are: welfare reform and active help to the unemployed; skill formation; wage flexibility; shorter hours and early retirement; flexibility of employment; and cuts in labour taxes.

The evidence reviewed here shows that the first three of these are crucial, but that the last three would make little difference. The general conclusion offered here is that the key to conquering unemployment is to make individuals more employable, improving their appeal to employers and letting their wages adjust to reflect productivity.

Our problems will not be solved through artificial rationing of work, nor through exposing workers to unrestricted "hire and fire" practices. Progress lies along a middle way between the unregulated labour market of North America and the overprotected system on the Continent. What is the evidence for this, and what exactly needs to be done? The best evidence comes from the wide variety of labour market institutions in different countries, and the wide variety of unemployment rates which accompany them. [1] It is thus useful to review the main institutions and their effects.

Welfare Reform and Help to the Unemployed

As is well known, unemployment in the U.S. has been lower than in most

European countries. But there is in fact no systematic difference in short-term unemployment. The real difference is in long-term unemployment, as shown in Table 11.1.

Table 11.1 Average Unemployment Rate, 1990s

	TOTAL	UNDER 1 YEAR	OVER 1 YEAR
USA	6.2	5.7	0.6
UK	8.9	5.5	3.4
Belgium	8.6	3.4	4.2
France	10.9	6.7	4.2
Germany	6.9	4.0	2.9
Italy	10.4	3.9	6.6
Netherlands	6.5	3.5	3.0
Norway	5.4	4.2	1.2
Spain	20.2	9.4	10.8
Sweden	6.0	5.2	0.8

Source: OEDC, Employment Outlook, various issues, 1990-96

Why is there the difference in average unemployment rates? The obvious explanation is that, in the U.S., unemployment insurance (for those who get it) runs out after six months, while in European countries it lasts for many years. Figure 11.1 illustrates the correlation among the maximum time for which one may collect unemployment (vertical axis) and the prevalence of long-term unemployment (horizontal axis). The positive relationship highlights that where benefits last long, unemployment lasts long. In other words, you get what you pay for. If you pay for inactivity, that is what you get.

There are two possible solutions in light of this obvious fact. One is the American route, or the heartless response: cut off the money. That would be a disaster for Europe. In America one sees the the emergence of a massive under-class, especially of men, as 2 percent of adult American men are in prison and 5 percent are on parole or probation. In fact, the employment rate in America in the 1990s as a fraction of prime aged men employed is no better than in Europe. Hence, a better solution would be to integrate this under-class into the workforce as opposed to cutting off benefits.

An alternative, more humane middle way would be to keep paying benefits, but after a period of unemployment pay only for activity rather than

Figure 11.1   Long-term Benefits and
Long-term Unemployment, 1989-94

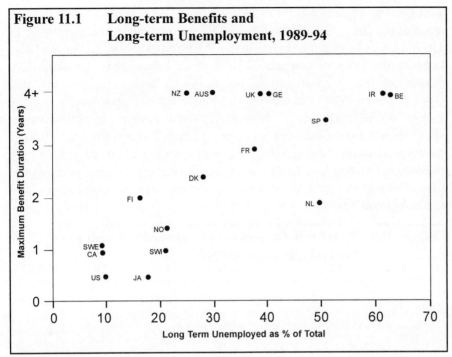

Source: OECD

inactivity. This will eliminate long-term unemployment. Long-term unemployment is a terrible waste because after a period unemployed people cease to be of interest to employers. Even if employers have vacancies, they are loath to hire the long-term unemployed. Thus, if the authorities try to expand the economy by stimulating demand, inflation can easily take off even when there are many people who are long-term unemployed. Thus long-term unemployment fails to serve the only purpose of unemployment, which is to restrain inflation. The answer, therefore, is to prevent people entering long-term unemployment in the first place.

For young people under 25, Britain has applied precisely this approach. After six months of unemployment they each enter a period of intensive counseling from which they will either get a job (unsubsidised) or choose one of three full-time activities: a subsidised job with a regular employer, work on an environmental or voluntary project, or full-time vocational education. They will no longer be able to draw benefits. If after further six months they have still not got a regular job, there will be another period of counselling.

This so-called "New Deal" is a major social experiment which could well become an example for other countries.[2] It is clearly in line with the spirit of the Guidelines adopted by the European leaders in Luxembourg in 1997. Europe has been fortunate in that the European Commission, and particularly the Director General of DG5, Alan Larson from Sweden, have pushed for this and Europe now has in the Guidelines the principle that there should be an offer of activity within a year to everybody and within six months for younger people. Specifically the Guidelines are that member states should ensure that: every unemployed adult is offered a new start in the form of a job, training, retraining, work practice or other employability measure before reaching twelve months of unemployment; and every unemployed young person is given such a new start before reaching six months of unemployment.

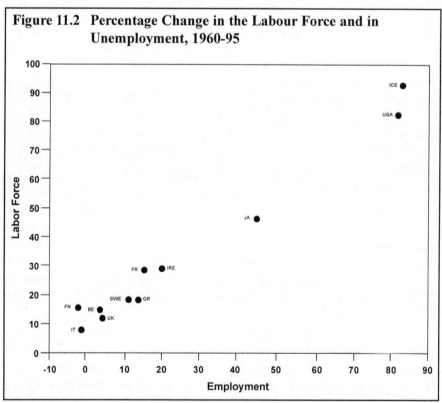

Figure 11.2   Percentage Change in the Labour Force and in Unemployment, 1960-95

Source: OEDC

This was an extremely important decision and probably the best hope for reducing unemployment in Europe. The unemployed are not, of course, the only group of working age who depend on welfare benefits.

There are also people on incapacity benefits and lone mothers. Many of these should really be working but the systems of passive hand-outs have encouraged them to become dependent on benefits. With more active help they could be found work. Britain is currently planning how to do this.

The obvious question about all these "Welfare to Work" policies is: "Where do the extra jobs come from?" The answer is that jobs do get created when the effective supply of labour increases. As Figure 11.2 shows, the volume of employment in a country does respond to the number of people who are seeking work. The mechanism is simple: if labour supply increases and the number of jobs does not, inflation starts falling and this makes possible an increase in aggregate demand, which in turn increases employment in line with the increase in labour supply.

But jobs only respond to what employers perceive as the effective supply of labour. If people have been long-term unemployed, their attractiveness to employers diminishes sharply and they can easily become effectively excluded from the world of work. Thus, by preventing long-term unemployment, one can expand the effective supply of labour and thus the number of jobs.

This course will lead to an expansion of employment at any particular level of inflation because if one expands the number of people who are really attractive to employers, one will have jobs. Many people may doubt this. The simplest example, however, is that of the Pilgrim Fathers landing at Cape Cod. There were no jobs, but when they landed jobs were created. The problem with long-term unemployment is that it had led to exclusion and people drifting on into a state where they are completely unattractive to employers, they perform no useful function, and their presence does nothing to contain inflation. It is a complete waste.

Skills

Another key dimension of employability is skills. In nearly all countries, unemployment rates for unqualified people are three to four times as high as for university graduates. This mismatch means that, when the economy expands, inflationary pressure develops in the skilled labour market and the expansion has to be halted while there is still intolerable unemployment among the unskilled.

The only solution is to increase the number of skilled people and by the same token reduce the number of unskilled. This is becoming increasingly urgent, for as trade grows between the West and the Third World, with its billions of unskilled workers, the demand for unskilled labour in the West will sharply decrease, except in a few service sectors. It is therefore important that every young person should acquire a serious level of skill.

Some countries have been particularly successful at this, especially those of continental Europe. There the supply of skilled labour has grown in line with the increase in demand (Layard, et. al, 1998). Even though there has been little change in wage differentials between skilled and unskilled, the unemployment rate of the unskilled has not in general risen relative to the skilled. Overall unemployment has grown for quite other reasons, discussed above.

In the United States, it is clear that the demand for skilled people has risen faster and the demand for unskilled people has fallen faster than the change in the pattern of skill levels in the labour force. As a result, wage differentials have increased enormously and the unemployment rate of unskilled people has risen relative to the skilled. In 1998 in the U.S. a white male whose wages are in the bottom tenth has a real wage which is half that of the equivalent German male.

Britain too has done badly in developing skills for the less academic half of the population (though very well for the top half). In consequence Britain also has experienced a massive fall in the relative wages of the unskilled. However, the Blair government has committed itself to securing a skill for every youngster. This is crucial. In addition, there is a commitment to "Lifelong Learning" to be achieved partly through a new "University for Industry", based on distance learning and developing skills at all levels. To achieve a skill for every youngster and to repair the drastic lack of skill among adults will require a major input of public money.

Thus, the Anglo-Saxon countries actually have a lot to learn from Europe. It remains the case that all are in a race against time. The demand for low-skilled workers will continue to decline even faster than it has in the past as trade with developing countries deepens. The future of low-skilled workers in the Group of Seven (G7) nations is so bleak that everything possible must be done to move them from that category.

Wage Flexibility

Where there is a mismatch between the pattern of demand and supply, wage adjustment is a crucial mechanism for maintaining employability. One dimension of wage structure is the skill differential. Another is the pattern of regional wage differences. Britain used to be famous for its regional unemployment, with much higher unemployment in Scotland, Wales and northern England than in the South. These differences have now largely gone, as relative wages have fallen in high unemployment areas and stimulated employment there.

On the Continent, changes in relative wages are much more difficult. Workers in the south of Italy or in eastern Germany have much more difficulty in pricing themselves into work. This is a key area for reform. Some, including the Organisation for Economic Cooperation Development (OECD), have concluded that there should be completely decentralized wage-setting. However, in societies where there are powerful and established unions, there is a great danger in a decentralized pay setting system as leap-frogging between unions may result. For countries in which unions participate in a coordinated process of wage negotiation there results less wage pressure than where there is decentralized wage setting with powerful unions. Thus, in regard to decentralization, caution is needed. In many countries of Europe, especially the Netherlands, Germany and Austria, the system of coordinated bargaining has a key role in securing wage moderation. Indeed, one dreads to think what inflationary pressures would have been in west Germany after the reunification shock if it had had a more decentralized system of wage determination.

The trick for these countries is how to maintain the discipline coming from co-ordination while at the same time changing relative wages across regions. It is quite apparent that in southern Italy, eastern Germany, eastern Belgium, and so on that there are high unemployment areas which are simply due to the insistence that people be paid wages similar in those areas as in the high-employment regions. This problem must be addressed in order to reduce unemployment in these regions.

Wage flexibility is desirable, but rising wage inequality is not. Hence, the employment characteristics of people in the labour pool should not be evolving in a way that has wage flexibility lead to greater wage inequality.

Conclusion on Solutions

These then are the key issues that need confronting if European unemployment is to be addressed. They are approaches based on helping individuals to be employable. They are, regrettably, very different from what many policymakers and commentators think to be the key solutions for unemployment. There are three other ideas, which are largely red herrings. In various ways all these other ideas assume that the problem of unemployment is one of inadequate demand. While that is true at various points in the business cycle, the long-term constraint on reducing unemployment is the tendency for inflation to rise when employers experience labour shortages. The following three ideas do nothing to address that problem.

Idea 1: Shorter Hours and Earlier Retirement

One proposal, supported by the left of centre French and Italian governments and by the German trade unions, is to reduce hours of work. This can make sense as a temporary measure in a recession but it will not reduce the sustainable level of unemployment.

Initially, of course, unemployment will fall since shorter hours for workers mean that more workers are required to produce the same level of output. But if one started from the sustainable level of unemployment, any lower level would produce inflationary pressures. The authorities would have to deflate the level of demand and one should end up with the same numbers in work as before. These people would be working shorter hours and producing less.

There is not a fixed amount of work to be done (or "lump of labour"). One can easily reduce the amount of work by foolish policies. All the evidence is that changes in hours of work have no effect on the sustainable unemployment rate (Nickell and Jackman, 1991). This, therefore, would be a disastrous route to go down if the aim is to reduce unemployment, in anything but the very short run. Likely one will get to a situation where if this comes into force in the countries mentioned above, it occurs at the peak of the boom when it would be the least appropriate time to do it.

A related policy, followed in many countries, especially Germany, is to get unemployment down by reducing the supply of labour through early retirement. Again, this would initially reduce unemployment. But that would then increase inflation and the authorities would act to reduce aggregate demand and employment. The number of jobs and the wealth of the country would fall.

Idea 2: Easier Dismissal

A second idea (coming from the right of centre, rather than the left of centre) is that if bosses could fire workers more easily, they would hire more people. This is of course true. But they would also fire more people. The evidence, accepted by most economists, is that these two effects would roughly cancel out. If sacking is easier, there is more short-term unemployment (due to more sacking), but less long-term unemployment (due to more hiring). Total unemployment is roughly unaffected. Male unemployment is higher (which is why it is relatively high in England) and female and youth unemployment are lower (which is why they are relatively low in England).

There may, of course, be productivity arguments for giving managers more power to sack people, though this does appear to reduce their tendency to train as many people as when they are stuck with them. But whatever its merits on productivity grounds, there is no reason to think that flexibility of employment (as opposed to flexibility of wages) would reduce total unemployment.

Idea 3: Cut Employers Payroll Taxes

A third idea is that employment is restricted through taxes on firms for the labour that they employ. These taxes are, of course, very high in many Continental European countries. But they are not what is limiting the demand for labour. Macroeconomic policy could always stimulate enough demand for labour if one were not worried about inflation. There is no convincing evidence that switching taxes from labour onto (say) products would affect the level of employment at which inflationary pressures develop.

The reason is that if there were a tax on products, workers would insist on higher wages, and labour costs would remain the same. There is, however, one important exception. If there is a high minimum wage, which prevents wages from adjusting to the employment tax, with a high employment tax on top of it, the tax can really cut the number of jobs available to minimum wage workers. Thus in France there is a strong case for the recent cuts in labour taxes for people close to the minimum wage.

Conclusion

In the very bad old days, people thought that unemployment could permanently be reduced by stimulating aggregate demand. This belief has died everywhere, in Britain in 1976 and in France in 1982.

In the not so bad old days that followed, a host of structural policies were proposed. Some still focused on demand side issues spreading a given amount of work, or stimulating job creation by employers. These ideas (1-3) did not address the fundamental problem: how to ensure that inflationary pressures do not develop while there are still massive pockets of unemployed people.

The only way to address this problem is to make all the unemployed attractive to employers through active help with motivation and job finding, through skill formation, and through a flexible system of wage differentials. Nothing else will do the trick.

Notes

1   The evidence is examined systematically in R. Jackman, R. Layard and S. Nickell (1996), "Combating Unemployment: Is Flexibility Enough?", *Macroeconomic Policies and Structural Reform,* OECD, Geneva.
2   From November, Britain will he piloting a similar approach for people over 25 years of age.

References

Jackman, R., Layard, R., Manacorda, M. and Petrongolo, B. (1998), "Understanding Skills Mismatch: Europe And The US Compared", London School of Economics and Political Science, mimeo, April.

Layard, R. (1998), "Employability", in M. Fraser (ed.), *The G8 & the World Economy,* Strategems Publishing Limited, London

Layard, R., Nickell, S. and Jackman, R. (1991), *Unemployment: Macroeconomic Performance and the Labour Market*, Oxford University Press, Oxford, p. 504.

12 Combating Transnational Financial Crime

GEORGE STAPLE, QC

KY2 (UK)

Fo 2

The International Challenge

Since the abolition of exchange control in the late 1970s and early 1980s, it has been possible instantly to transfer money of any amount or denomination virtually anywhere in the world. This means that, because criminal law is territorially based, and differs across jurisdictions, the investigation and prosecution of fraud and the related offences of money laundering and corruption are particularly dependent upon mutual legal assistance between states. Although many of the cases that have attracted attention in Britain in the 1990s are so-called "City frauds", the authorities are dealing increasingly with very determined international criminals, who have taken to fraud and related offences as an easy way of making money.

The activities of these criminals usually span several jurisdictions. They have no regard for international frontiers. Indeed they are adept at exploiting the territorial nature of national laws. There is ample scope for the commission of offences partly in one jurisdiction and partly in others. Often witnesses, such as bankers and professional advisers, together with the documentary evidence, are to be found in a number of different jurisdictions. Suspects are frequently not in the jurisdiction in which they should be brought to trial. The proceeds of the crime can be in yet another jurisdiction, while the victims, who are seldom remembered in the criminal justice system, can be somewhere else again.

For example, in May of 1997, the former shipping magnate Abbas Gokal was sentenced at the Old Bailey in London to fourteen years imprisonment for masterminding a massive swindle involving £750 million in loans from the Bank of Credit and Commerce International (BCCI). Investigators from the Serious Fraud Office (SFO) of the British Government visited no fewer than 19 countries on a tour that included the USA, Pakistan, Grand Cayman, Monaco, Abu Dhabi and the Isle of Man. Prosecutions arising out of the collapse of BCCI were brought in a number of jurisdictions. In a second example, the Maxwell case, at one time there were no fewer than 100 police officers, lawyers and accountants working in the case team. The investigators visited 20 different jurisdictions. Contemporary commercial fraud has thus become fully global in many ways.

There have so far been few cases in Britain involving Russian crime that have gone through the rather lengthy process of investigation and concluded with a trial. Yet Russia is a rich country and there is the opportunity for criminal activity there, as there are in other rich countries. All should be very much on guard against the possibility of international frauds and the related offence of money laundering involving Russia and many other countries.

International trade, having been a feature of life for many centuries, has led to the development of a body of private international law that has ensured the efficient disposal of cross border disputes between commercial people. But large-scale international fraud is a relatively new phenomenon. While acknowledging the economic advantages of the abolition of exchange control and the development of information technology, the international community now needs to ask how well prepared it is to deal with the huge expansion of international fraud that comes with these developments. On the whole, it has been rather ill prepared.

The British and G8 Response

The belated response of governments to this increasingly difficult problem can be seen in the approach of the British Government, responsible for one of the world's major financial centres. Governments take the view that their financial services industries are very important. They should be effectively protected by a strong system of regulation in order to prevent fraud and by a strong system of investigation and prosecution to deal with fraud when it gets through the regulatory net.

In spite of the decline of sterling as a reserve currency, the City of London accounts for some seven percent of the United Kingdom's (UK) gross domestic product. It is a leading centre of global currency and capital markets. There are more foreign banks in London than anywhere else in the world. London has overtaken New York and Tokyo as the leading fund management centre. *The Financial Times* has estimated that between 40% and 50% of the world's international mergers and acquisitions are handled through the City. At the same time, successive governments have encouraged ordinary families to invest their savings in the equity markets, and make personal provision for their pensions.

The City of London financial district - the Square Mile - is therefore a vital component, not only of the UK's financial system, but also of the international financial system. Its reputation is a precious thing that should not be taken for granted. Unless that reputation can be protected, the City's standing as a financial centre will quickly decline. It needs effective laws and strong guardians to enforce those laws. This approach conditions the British government's policy to financial services at home, abroad, and in Britain's offshore jurisdictions.

Much attention is being devoted to financial regulation. Within three weeks of taking office in May 1997, the new British Labour Government, through the Chancellor of the Exchequer, announced a total restructuring of the regulatory regime. When complete it will bring to an end the system of self-regulation that has so far existed. Moreover, the Government made it clear that it was no less concerned about the law relating to the investigation and prosecution of fraud and money laundering.

The British Home Office is consulting on the continued use of juries in cases of serious fraud. It announced in April 1998 that the Home Secretary had asked the Law Commission to review the law on fraud. The Commission has been asked to consider whether the law is adequate for effective prosecution, is fair to potential defendants and, importantly, whether the law meets the needs of developing technology, including electronic means of transfer. In particular, the Commission has been asked to consider whether a general offence of fraud, which Britain still does not have, would improve the criminal law.

The British Government recognises that successful investigation and prosecution is reliant on a network of treaties, conventions and bilateral agreements. These impose a further legal regime not usually encountered in the prosecution of other crime. To ensure that this system works effectively, the Government knows that it needs the co-operation of other states. That will not be forthcoming unless it readily responds to requests for help itself.

This was very much the policy of John Major's Conservative government in Britain. That policy has been reiterated by the successor Labour government of Tony Blair. Indeed international crime is high on its list of domestic priorities, and of those for the UK's Presidency of the European Union, where it has worked through the Action Plan to Combat Organised Crime. It was one of the major subjects for discussion at the May 1998 G8 summit in Birmingham. Meeting in London the week before the Birmingham summit, the G7 Finance Ministers agreed to expand the membership of the Financial Action Task Force (FATF) and to encourage the development of further regional anti-money laundering bodies.

With this level of political commitment, any jurisdiction which claims to offer sophisticated financial services must subscribe to a strict regime to prevent, detect and investigate fraud and money laundering in its own territory. It must also subscribe to a network of treaties which enable it to give maximum assistance to foreign investigators. In Europe, the Convention on Mutual Legal Assistance in Criminal Matters of 1959 enables evidence to be gathered in one Contracting State for use in the criminal courts of another. It was not brought into effect in the United Kingdom until 1991. It has enormously improved the response to international fraud throughout Europe.

However, although many countries now have modern mutual assistance laws, others still rely on old legislation not designed to assist with fraud investigation. Where the relationship between the UK and the overseas territories is closest, the mutual assistance arrangements may be most constrained. If, for example, Britain asks for help from Switzerland, its request will usually be acted upon swiftly under the European Convention, through the medium of an examining magistrate. But if a similar request goes to certain of Britain's dependent territories, which are often significant offshore financial centres in their own right, it is rejected unless and until a defendant has been charged. A number of investigations have had to be abandoned as a result. Very simply, it has proved impossible to gather sufficient evidence to charge someone without first being able to carry out the investigation in the overseas territory. From time to time that assistance has been refused.

In order to offer reciprocity, the UK has done much to improve its own legal regime. It has tried to ensure a rapid response to the requests of other states. But however much it does to ensure that an immediate response to a request for help can be made, this does not always mean that the foreign state will reciprocate. Often a response will depend critically on the state of personal relations between the individuals who are responsible at each end.

British Assistance in International Investigations

The powers under Section 2 of the Criminal Justice Act of 1987, which enables the Director of the Serious Fraud Office to compel the production of information in cases of serious or complex fraud in England, Wales and Northern Ireland, have been extended so that the SFO can assist fraud investigations being conducted by foreign authorities. This development has enormously improved relations between the UK and states concerned with international investigations.

The powers may be used to obtain information not only from those who may be under investigation, but also from third parties who may be subject to some obligation or duty that prevents them from providing the information voluntarily. Professional advisers and banks are the leading examples. Failure to comply is a criminal offence, as is the destruction of documents known to be the subject of an investigation.

During the period covered by the SFO's 1997 Annual Report, 144 notices under Section 2 were issued on behalf of overseas governments. The Office received requests from as far afield as Argentina and the Ukraine. For instance, in November 1996 the SFO agreed to a request from the French criminal authorities to investigate allegations of market manipulation involving Eurotunnel shares. The investigation followed a report from the Commission des Opérations de Bourse that alleged that several banks concerned in underwriting Eurotunnel shares had sold shares ahead of the public launch. Three weeks later an English national was questioned by the SFO about his role in the management of millions of pounds belonging to a Norwegian shipping magnate. The Norwegian authorities had asked the SFO to conduct the British end of an international criminal enquiry into alleged fraud and tax evasion.

The case that aroused most attention involved the former Italian Prime Minister Silvio Berlusconi. The SFO had been asked to assist the Italian authorities that were conducting a criminal enquiry into the removal of £51 million from Mr Berlusconi's multi-national company Fininvest SpA. The Italian investigators alleged that the monies had been used for unlawful purposes, which, so it was alleged, included the making of illicit payments to Italian politicians. The Italian authorities wanted the British Government, via the SFO, to assist them in obtaining documents held at the Regent Street offices of a company that was said to have been ultimately owned by a Swiss bank. Mr. Berlusconi and Fininvest challenged the actions of the Home Secretary and the SFO in the High Court, alleging that the Italian request for assistance was an extensive fishing expedition which the Home Secretary had no jurisdiction to entertain or refer to the SFO. In the end the Divisional Court rejected this argument and found in favour of the Home Office and the SFO.

British Assistance in Evidence for Trial

There can be real difficulties in international cases when they move on to trial. Bankers and others often have to be brought from abroad to explain the intricacies of financial transactions involving networks of bank accounts and the use of offshore companies, trusts and administrators. However, such witnesses cannot be forced to attend British courts. They may even be subject to strict secrecy laws with penal sanctions in their own country if they do. It is difficult to imagine a greater inhibition to successful prosecution.

There are provisions in Britain's 1987 Criminal Justice Act which allow the admission of hearsay in the form of business and other records without a witness to produce and explain them. This is in response to cases where it is not possible to bring witnesses to Britain from abroad or to take their evidence by satellite link. Unfortunately insufficient use has been made of these provisions, probably due to the strength of the oral tradition in British courts, and in other legal systems which adhere to the common law tradition. Judges tend to feel that, especially in respect of important witnesses, the jury should see and hear the witness in person in the witness box. The simple production of written documents has not been considered good enough. But there are signs that that view is changing.

Good use has also been made of satellite technology in taking live evidence from overseas witnesses. One case involved eight witnesses from Canada and Australia attending studios in their own countries and being examined and cross-examined live on a television screen in a London court. Their contribution was essential to a satisfactory outcome of the case. If they had not been willing to take part in the link up, that might well have been the end of the matter.

There is a real need for an international treaty to compel overseas witnesses to give evidence to the Court live by satellite. The court of trial needs to be able to send a request to an overseas jurisdiction asking that a witness be required to give evidence by satellite. This must be done in the knowledge that the witness will be compelled to attend a studio for the purpose of a live transmission of his or her evidence to the court of trial. Appropriately, at the meeting of Justice and Interior Ministers of the G8 in December 1997, the communiqué expressed the Ministers' agreement to intensify their efforts to use video-link technology as a means of securing testimony from witnesses located abroad.

International Co-operation in Investigations

Effectively to address borderless crime, a concerted effort at international co-operation is required. The investigating and prosecuting authorities in the

UK take their relationships with overseas authorities very seriously. They place much emphasis on developing experience and expertise in dealing with foreign jurisdictions. The UK authorities have also co-operated at home with overseas law enforcement agencies and judicial authorities wherever possible. There is no substitute for good working and personal relationships between those responsible in the different jurisdictions. Colleagues overseas also subscribe to this view.

In general, in the common law countries where investigations are in the hands of the police or customs authorities, the UK enforcement authorities can arrange for their overseas counterparts to carry out enquiries on their behalf. They can even arrange to carry them out themselves together with a foreign law enforcement officer. Help from Interpol, and more recently Europol, has proved particularly valuable. However, where a witness has to be compelled to provide evidence on commission, more formal procedures are necessary. These will depend upon the terms of the appropriate mutual legal assistance treaty, convention or agreement.

In civil law countries, very little investigation is possible, other than through the courts and the system of examining magistrates. In Switzerland, for example, the local police may attempt to establish the whereabouts of a person, check the central hotel register or make informal enquiries of a witness. However, they can do little else without the sanction of an examining magistrate.

The United Kingdom is party to an impressive range of international instruments dealing with drug trafficking, money laundering and organised crime. These instruments include: the European Convention on Mutual Assistance in Criminal Matters 1959; the 1978 Additional Protocol to that Convention; the Scheme relating to Mutual Assistance in Criminal Matters within the Commonwealth; the United Nations Convention against the Illicit Traffic in Narcotic Drugs and Psychotropic Substances 1988 (the Vienna Convention); and, the Council of Europe Convention on Laundering, Search, Seizure and Confiscation of the Proceeds of Crime 1990. In addition, the UK is party to both bilateral and multilateral treaties and memoranda made with many other jurisdictions.

The ability of UK law enforcement agencies to give mutual assistance is not confined simply to countries covered by these agreements. Nor does the UK require bilateral treaties or agreements before such help can be given. Judges, magistrates, public prosecutors, police officers and defence lawyers from the requesting state will normally be allowed to be present when the evidence is taken and may be allowed to put questions to the person giving evidence.

The UK will not compel someone residing in the UK to travel abroad for the purpose of giving evidence in another state's courts. A witness must always consent to appear as a witness abroad. Even prisoners in UK jails, where they consent, and where satisfactory security arrangements can be made, will be allowed to go abroad to give evidence. A convention on evidence by satellite link would ensure that this evidence is available to the court of trial.

Moreover, it is now possible to obtain search warrants on premises in the UK in respect of foreign investigations. There are, of course, the special provisions in fraud cases noted above. The same procedures as those used for domestic UK cases will apply. The requirements of UK law are detailed and reflect the safeguards which Parliament deems necessary in what is clearly a sensitive area for the exercise of search powers.

The UK rarely refuses to assist other states. But refusal may be made on political, security or national interest grounds. It may also be unavoidable in certain other cases, for example, where evidence is protected by legal professional privilege or where the legal requirements for search and seizure powers are not met.

Over the last 300 years the courts have consistently affirmed the limitations on the ability of government authorities to search private premises and require the production of incriminating material. As Lord Chief Justice Camden said long ago in the case of Entick v. Carrington, "If a messenger of the Government sets foot on private property without the owner's consent, he must justify it by law. The issue of a search warrant is a very serious interference with the liberty of the subject". It is important that these basic freedoms be respected during the immense complexities of an international criminal investigation.

A further issue concerns extradition. The law of extradition needs constant vigilance. There are too many countries that refuse to extradite their own nationals. Sometimes they refuse to extradite because they assert a world-wide jurisdiction over their own nationals, on the principle that the home state will prosecute them wherever they commit their crimes. This reluctance to extradite is no longer appropriate when so many legal systems have incorporated universally recognised safeguards of human rights. There is no reason to fear that an accused will not be treated fairly in most countries that might request his or her extradition to face trial. There may be some where that will be the case, and the refusal to extradite may still be justified. However, it will not be very many.

The present extradition procedures are simply outdated and inadequate to meet the challenge presented by cross border crime. They are still mainly dependent on bilateral arrangements that derive mainly from treaties concluded in the late nineteenth century. There are some regional treaties, for instance within the Commonwealth and Western Europe. Yet, they fall a very long way short of covering the whole world. The time has come for a fresh and bolder approach with a new arrangement on a global scale. Such global schemes have been successful and effective in other areas of international activity, notably aviation and shipping.

A global scheme on extradition should also be established. The United Nations Model Treaty on Extradition, intended as a guide in the drafting of treaties, would be a useful starting point. However, one weakness is that it fails to address fully the procedures for extradition, leaving them to be addressed by states in their domestic and enabling legislation.

Money Laundering

No one knows with certainty how much money derived from drug trafficking, fraud, pornography, prostitution, smuggling and corruption is laundered every year through the financial system. Estimates vary from $500 billion to $1,000 billion. It could be much more. Yet it is clear that money laundering is now on such a scale that it could begin to undermine some national economies and threaten the stability of the world's financial system. British Foreign Secretary Robin Cook's speech in Kuala Lumpur in August 1997, which emphasised that the British Government would focus resources on the money laundering systems which lie at the heart of drug trafficking, was thus very welcome.

Sophisticated financial centres such as the City of London, where it is possible to trade in any conceivable commodity or instrument, are particularly attractive to the launderers. Shares and other investments are obvious routes. Property and works of art are also attractive.

The UK possesses not only a wide variety of ways to clean money, but also a formidable battery of laws to prevent money laundering. One can go to prison for up to 14 years with an unlimited fine for committing the offence of money laundering. One can go to prison for up to five years with an unlimited fine for failing to report a suspicious transaction. However, if the launderer does manage to avoid detection and process ill-gotten gains through the UK financial system, he or she will have achieved a very high standard of cleanliness.

Some suggest that there is often a link between tax offences, tax frauds, and money laundering but that the important principle of confidentiality of tax matters makes exchange of information difficult. The original anti-money laundering legislation in Europe did not cover tax evasion. There is now legislation being put in place that will cover that throughout Europe. It is already in place in the UK. The old principle of not providing foreign authorities with information about peoples' tax affairs is to some extent breached now where money laundering is concerned.

Professional advisers must be on their guard. It is not by any means certain that the professions are generally aware of the scale of the problem and the vulnerability of their position. In particular, lawyers are needed to carry out and document transactions when money is laundered. They must satisfy themselves as to the true identity of those for whom they are acting. It is no longer sufficient for money simply to turn up from a Swiss bank account held by a Panamanian company. Rigorous checks must now be made. Fortunately banks are very much more alert to the possibility of being used as a laundry than was once the case.

Reports of suspicious transactions to the National Criminal Intelligence Service were running by 1998 at slightly under 16,000 a year. With this level of reporting, criminals are likely to take their money to less demanding regimes. These countries must therefore quickly bring themselves up to the same level of prevention as the richest countries. As a minimum, in line with the recommendations of the Financial Action Task Force (FATF), all states should bring into force laws which make money laundering, and failure to disclose knowledge or suspicion of it, specific offences. It should also be possible to obtain restraint and forfeiture orders throughout the world. All states should make it an offence to help someone retain the proceeds in the knowledge or suspicion that they have been obtained from criminal activities.

To achieve this requires very considerable political will and the deployment of resources on the part of international organisations (in particular by formulating model laws) and on the part of governments throughout the world. If the commitment is not made, however, criminal activity will continue to grow, because those responsible will be able to conceal or disguise the proceeds of their crimes and to spend them with impunity.

Perhaps the nadir in money laundering legislation was reached when the Seychelles government passed an extraordinary law that effectively turned this independent Commonwealth country into a haven for international criminals. It offered foreign investors immunity from prosecution by any police force in the world in exchange for a payment of $10 million. This "subscription" would give such "investors" diplomatic status and Seychelles citizenship. Further the government would guarantee their assets on the islands if foreign authorities tried to seize them. The government also offered economic and fiscal incentives when further investments were made. Such was the international outrage that greeted this piece of legislation that it was quickly repealed.

The Seychelles is a small place and perhaps in itself not so important. There are only so many big international criminals who could find accommodation on the Seychelles if they wanted to take advantage of the law the Seychelles' authorities were proposing to introduce. Yet there are a very large number of small countries, and some not so small, who have virtually no laws regarding money laundering. They have done virtually nothing to introduce anti-money laundering regimes. The May 1998 decision by the G8 finance ministers to enlarge the FATF specifically to encourage anti-money laundering bodies to be established in areas of the world which hitherto have not worried much about money laundering, is a response to that concern. The more the developed nations tighten up on their anti-money laundering laws, the more criminals will be driven to other regimes. This is the moment to ensure that the other regimes in the smaller countries are equipped to deal with these individuals as well.

Conclusion

The international community is now much better served by instruments designed to provide international co-operation. In particular, in those areas that span all crimes such as extradition and mutual legal assistance for gathering evidence, the initiatives taken within Europe are impressive. It has shown a lead that other areas of the world have, as a result, taken up. However, much more could and should be done. There are lacunae that need to be filled. Misunderstandings between governments still arise and must be addressed. Principles of sovereignty mean that borderless investigation will not in the foreseeable future be possible. International co-operation must thus be the means to meet the challenge of the transnational criminal. The G8 is well positioned to continue to provide leadership in securing such co-operation.

Bibliography

Aghion, P. and Tirole, J. (1997), "Formal and Real Authority in Organizations", *Journal of Political Economy*, 105(1).

Baker, A. (1996), "The Historical Development of the G-7: An Incoherent and Disjointed Response to Global Interdependence?", *G7RU Working Paper No. 2,* School of Public Policy, Economics and Law, University of Ulster, Jordanstown, Northern Ireland.

Bayne, N. (1992), "The Course of Summitry", *The World Today,* vol. 48, no. 2.

Bayne, N. (1995), "The G7 Summit and the Reform of Global Institutions", *Government and Opposition,* vol. 30, no. 4.

Bayne, N. (1998), "Britain, the G8 and the Commonwealth: Lessons of the Birmingham Summit", *The Round Table,* no. 348.

Bergsten, F. C. (1998), "The Great War: The Euro vs. The Dollar", *The International Economy,* (May/June).

Bergsten, F. C. and Henning, C. R. (1996), *Global Economic Leadership and the Group of Seven,* Institute for International Economics, Washington, D.C.

Blackburn, K. and Christensen, M. (1989), "Monetary Policy and Policy Credibility", *Journal of Economic Literature,* vol. 27.

Brewer, T. L. and Young, S. (1995), "The Multilateral Agenda for Foreign Direct Investment: Problems, Principles and Priorities for Negotiation at the OECD and WTO", *World Competition* 18 (4).

Brewer, T. L. and Young, S. (1998), *Multilateral Investment Rules and Multinational Enterprises,* Oxford University Press, Oxford.

Caiola, M. (1995), *A Manual For Country Economists,* Training Series Number 1, Volume 1, International Monetary Fund.

Camdessus, M. and Wolfensohn, J. D. (1998), "The Bretton Woods Institutions: Responding to the Asian Financial Crisis", in M. Fraser (ed.), *The G8 and the World Economy,* Strategems Publishing Ltd., London.

Centre for Economic Performance (1998), "Employability and Exclusion: What Governments Can Do", Papers from a Conference held on 6 May 1998 by the Centre for Economic Performance and the London School of Economics, London.

Chang, R. and Velasco, A. (1998), "The Asian Liquidity Crisis", Federal Reserve Bank of Atlanta, Working Paper 98-11.

Chayes, A. and Chayes, A. H. (forthcoming), *The New Sovereignty: Compliance with International Regulatory Agreements.*

Clarke, T. and Barlow, M. (1997), *MAI: The Multilateral Agreement on Investment and the Threat to Canadian Sovereignty,* Stoddart, Toronto.

Commission on Global Governance (1995), *Our Global Neighbourhood: The Report of the Commission on Global Governance,* Oxford University Press, New York.

Daniels, J. (1993), *The Meaning and Reliability of Economic Summit Undertakings, 1975-1989,* Garland Publishing, New York.

Daniels, J. P. and VanHoose D. D. (1999), *International Monetary and Financial Economics,* International Thompson Press / SouthWestern Publishing, Cincinnati.

De Silguy, Y. (1997), "The Impact of the Creation of the Euro on Financial Markets and the International Monetary System", address to the Institute of International Finance, Washington, Tuesday, 29 April.

Deibert, R. (1997), *Parchment, Printing and Hypermedia: Communication in World Order Transformation,* Columbia University Press, New York.

Dobson, W. (1991), "Economic Policy Coordination: Requiem or Prologue?" *International Economics,* vol. 30, Institute for International Economics, Washington, D.C.

Doran, C. (1985), *Forgotten Partnership,* Johns Hopkins, Baltimore.

Fitzgerald, E. V. K. (1998), "The Development Implications of the Multilateral Agreement on Investment", an independent study for the Department for International Development of the United Kingdom, Queen Elizabeth House, Oxford.

G7 Research Group (1998a), *The 1997 G7 Compliance Report,* G7 Research Group, University of Toronto (available at www.g7.utoronto.ca), Toronto.

G7 Research Group, (1998b), *The 1998 G7 Compliance Report,* G8 Research Group, University of Toronto (available at www.g7.utoronto.ca), Toronto.

Gestrin, M. and Rugman, A. (1996), "The NAFTA Investment Provisions: Prototype for Multinational Investment Rules" in P. Sauvé and A. B. Zampetti (eds.), *Market Access after the Uruguay Round: Investment, Competition and Technology Perspectives,* OECD, Paris.

Glick, R. (1998), "Capital Flows and Exchange Rates in the Pacific Basin", Federal Reserve Bank of San Francisco Economic Letter, #98-22.

Glick, R. and Rose, A. (1998), "How Do Currency Crises Spread?", Federal Reserve Bank of San Francisco Economic Letter, #98-25.

Goldstein, M. and Turner, P. (1996), "Banking Crises in Emerging Economies: Origins and Policy Options", *BIS Economic Papers,* No. 46.

Graham, E. M. (1996), "Investment and the New Multilateral Trade Context", in P. Sauvé and A. B. Zampetti (eds.), *Market Access after the Uruguay Round: Investment, Competition and Technology Perspectives,* OECD, Paris.

Hale, D. (1998), "What the Asian Crisis Is All About", *The International Economy,* (January/February).

Henning, R. (1996), "Europe's Monetary Union and the United States", *Foreign Policy* 102 (Spring).

Hodges, M. (1994), "More Efficiency, Less Dignity: British Perspectives on the Future Role and Working of the G7", *The International Spectator,* 29(2).

Hormats, R.D. (1998), "Commanding Thoughts", *The International Economy,* (January/February).

Ikenberry, J. (1993), "Salvaging the G-7", *Foreign Affairs* 72 (Spring).

Ionescu, G. (1995), "Reading Notes, Summer 1995: From International to Global Reform", *Government and Opposition* 30.

Jackman, R., Layard, R., Manacorda, M. and Petrongolo, B. (1998), "Understanding Skills Mismatch: Europe and the US Compared", London School of Economics and Political Science, mimeo, April.

Jacobson, H. K. and Weiss, E. B. (1995), "Strengthening Compliance with International Environmental Accords: Preliminary Observations from a Collaborative Project", *Global Governance,* vol.1, No. 2, May-August.

Jayawardena, L. (1989), "World Economic Summits: The Role of Representative Groups in the Governance of the World Economy", *Journal of the Society for International Development , vol.* 4.

Julius, D. (1998), "Trade and Investment in the Light of the Asian Crisis", *Bank of England Quarterly Bulletin,* vol. 38, no. 3.

Kenen, P. (ed) (1996), "From Halifax to Lyon: What Has Been Done about Crisis Management?", Essays in *International Finance,* #200, International Finance Section, Princeton University.

Kindleberger, C. (1973), *The World in Depression, 1929-39,* University of California Press, Berkley.

Kirton, J. (1989), "The Seven Power Summit as an International Concert", Paper presented at the International Studies Association Annual meeting, London, England, April.

Kirton, J. (1993), "The Seven Power Summit and the New Security Agenda", In D. Dewitt, D. Haglund and J. Kirton, (eds.), *Building a New Global Order: Emerging Trends in International Security,* Oxford University Press, Toronto.

Kirton, J. (1994), "Exercising Concerted Leadership: Canada's Approach to Summit Reform", *The International Spectator*, vol. 29 (April-June).

Kirton, J. (1995a), "The G-7, the Halifax Summit, and International Financial System Reform", *North American Outlook*, vol. 5 (June).

Kirton, J. (1995b), "The Diplomacy of Concert: Canada, the G7 and the Halifax Summit", *Canadian Foreign Policy*, vol. 3 (Spring).

Kirton, J. (1997a), "Canada and APEC: Contributions and Challenges", *Asia Pacific Papers*, vol. 3 (May).

Kirton, J. (1997b), "Le Role du G7 sur le Couple Integration Regionale/Security Globale", *Etudes Internationales*, vol. 28 (Juin).

Kirton, J. (1999), "Economic Co-operation: Summitry, Institutions and Structural Change" in G. Boyd and J. Dunning, (eds.), *Structural Change in the Global Economy,* Edward Elgar, Cheltenham.

Kirton, J. and Kokotsis, E. (1997), "Revitalizing the G-7: Prospects for the 1998 Birmingham Summit of the Eight", *International Journal*, vol. 53 (Winter 1997-8).

Kokotsis, E. (1998), *National Compliance with G7 Environment and Development Commitments, 1988-1995,* Ph.D. Dissertation, University of Toronto.

Kokotsis, E. (forthcoming 1999), *Promises Kept: National Compliance with G7 Environment and Development Commitments: 1988-95,* Garland Publishing, New York.

Kokotsis, E. and Kirton, J. (1997), "National Compliance with Environmental Regimes: The Case of the G7, 1988-1995", Paper prepared for the Annual Convention of the International Studies Association, Toronto, March 18-22.

Labbohm, H. (1995), "G7 Economic Summits: A View from the Lowlands", Netherlands Institute of International Relations, Clingendal, The Hague.

Lawrence, R. Z. (1996), "Towards Globally Contestable Markets", in P. Sauvé and A. B. Zampetti (eds.), *Market Access after the Uruguay Round: Investment, Competition and Technology Perspectives,* OECD, Paris.

Lawrence, R.Z., Bressand, A. and Ito, T. (1996), *A Vision for the World Economy,* Brookings Institute, Washington, D.C.

Layard, R. (1998), "Employability" in M. Fraser (ed.), *The G8 & the World Economy,* Strategems Publishing Limited, London.

Layard, R. and Nickell, S. (1996), "Combating Unemployment: Is Flexibility Enough?", *Macroeconomic Policies and Structural Reform,* OECD, Geneva.

Layard, R., Nickell, S. and Jackman, R. (1991), *Unemployment: Macroeconomic Performance and the Labour Market,* Oxford University Press, London.

Lewis, F. (1991-2), "The G-71/2 Directorate", *Foreign Policy* 85 (Winter).

Lindgren, C., Gillian, G. and Saal, M. (1996), "Bank Soundness and Macroeconomic Policy", *International Monetary Fund,* Washington, D.C.

Malmgren, H. B. (1998), "Dark Clouds Over Russia?", *The International Economy,* (January/February).

Merlini, C. (ed.) (1994), "The Future of the G-7 Summits", *The International Spectator,* vol. 29 (April-June).

Mitchell, R. B. (1994), *Intentional Oil Pollution at Sea: Environmental Policy and Treaty Compliance,* MIT Press, Cambridge, Mass.

Mulford, D. (1998), "Mulford Memorandum", *The International Economy,* (January/February).

Nye, J. and Keohane, R. (1977), *Power and Interdependence,* Little Brown, Boston.

Odom, W. (1995), "How to Create a True World Order", *Orbis* 39 (Spring).

Ostry, S. (1997), *The Post-Cold War Trading System: Who's on First?,* University of Chicago Press, Chicago.

Paarlberg, R. (1997), "Agricultural Policy Reform and the Uruguay Round: Synergistic Linkage in a Two-Level Game?" *International Organization,* vol. 51(3).

Putnam, R. (1989), " Diplomacy and Domestic Politics: The logic of Two-Level Games", *International Organization,* vol. 42.

Putnam, R. and Bayne, N. (1987), *Hanging Together: Cooperation and Conflict in the Seven-Power Summits,* 2nd edition, Sage Publications, London.

Putnam, R. and Henning, C. R. (1989), "The Bonn Summit of 1978: A Case Study in Coordination", in R. N. Cooper, B. Eichengreen, G. Holtham, R. D. Putnam and C. R. Henning (eds.), *Can Nations Agree?,* Brookings Institution, Washington, D.C.

Reinalda, B. and Verbeek, B. (eds.) (1998), *Autonomous Policy Making by International Organizations,* Routledge, London and New York; especially, Bayne, N., "International Economic Organizations: More Policy Making, Less Autonomy".

"Review and Outlook", *The Wall Street Journal* (15 September 1998), pp. A22.

Rugman, A. M. (1994), (ed.) *Foreign Investment and NAFTA,* University of South Carolina Press, Columbia, S.C.

Rugman, A. M. (1996), *Multinational Enterprises and Trade Policy,* Elgar, Cheltenham.

Rugman, A. M. (1997), "New Rules for Multinational Investment", *The International Executive* 39 (1).

Rugman, A. M. and D'Cruz, J. (1997a), "Strategies of Multinational Enterprises and Governments: The Theory of The Flagship Firm", in G. Boyd and A. M. Rugman (eds.), *Euro-Pacific Investment and Trade: Strategies and Structural Interdependencies,* Elgar, Cheltenham.

Rugman, A. M. and Gestrin, M. (1996), "A Conceptual Framework for a Multilateral Agreement on Investment: Learning from the NAFTA", in P. Sauvé and D. Schwanen (eds.), *Investment Rules for the Global Economy,* C.D. Howe Institute, Toronto.

Rugman, A., Kirton, J. and Soloway, J. (1999), *Environmental Regulations and Corporate Strategy: A NAFTA Perspective,* Oxford University Press, Oxford.

Sachs, J. (1998), "Global Capitalism: Making it Work", *The Economist,* 12 September.

Safarian, A. E. (1993), *Multinational Enterprises and Public Policy,* Elgar, Cheltenham.

Smith, A. (1995), "The Development of a Multilateral Agreement on Investment at the OECD: A Preview", in C. J. Green and T. L. Brewer (eds.) *Investment Issues in Asia and the Pacific Rim,* Oceana, Dobbs Ferry, New York.

Smyser, W. R. (1993), "Goodbye, G-7", *The Washington Quarterly,* vol. 16, No. 1.

Soros, G. (1998), "The Crises of Global Capitalism", *The Wall Street Journal,* 15 September.

Strange, S. (1987), *States and Markets: An Introduction to International Political Economy,* Pinter, London.

Strange, S. (1995), "The Limits of Politics", *Government and Opposition,* vol. 30, no. 3.

Ul Haq, M. (1994), "The Bretton Woods Institutions and Global Governance", in Peter Kenen, (ed.) *Managing the World Economy,* Institute for International Economics, Washington, D.C.

United Nations (1997), *World Investment Report 1997,* UNCTAD, Geneva.

USTR (1997), United States, United States Trade Representative, Study on the Operation and Effects of the North American Free Trade Agreement, July 1.

von Furstenberg, G., and Daniels, J.P. (1991), "Policy Undertakings by the Seven Summit Countries: Ascertaining the Degree of Compliance", Carnegie-Rochester Conference Series on Public Policy, 35.

von Furstenberg, G. and Daniels, J.P. (1992), *Economic Summit Declarations, 1975-1989: Examining the Written Record of International Cooperation,* Princeton Studies in International Finance, Princeton University Press, New Jersey.

Von Hagen, J. and Fratianni, M. (1998), "Banking Regulation with Variable Geometry", in B. Eichengreen and J. Frieden (eds.), *Forging an Integrated Europe,* The University of Michigan Press.

Wallace, W. (1984), "Political Issues at the Summits: A New Concert of Powers?", in C. Merlini (ed), *Economic Summits and Western Decision-Making,* Croom Helm, London & Sydney.

Weintraub, S. (1997), *NAFTA at Three: A Progress Report,* The Centre for Strategic and International Studies, Washington, D.C.

Whyman, W. E. (1995), "We Can't Go On Meeting Like This: Revitalizing the G-7 Process", *The Washington Quarterly* 18 (Summer).

Williamson, J. and Miller, M. (1987), "Targets and Indicators: A Blueprint for the International Coordination of Economic Policy", *Policy Analyses in International Economics* 22, Institute for International Economics, Washington, D.C.

Winham, G. and Grant, H. A. (1997), "Designing Institutions for Global Economic Co-operation: Investment and the WTO", Paper for Halifax Pre-G7 Summit Conference, May 1995, in G. Boyd and A. M. Rugman, (eds.), *Euro-Pacific Investment and Trade: Strategies and Structural Interdependencies,* Edward Elgar, Brookfield, VT.

Yoshitomi, M. (1995), "Main Issues of Macroeconomic Coordination: The Peso, Dollar and Yen Problems", 35-59, in S. Ostry and G. R. Winham, (eds.) *The Halifax Summit: Issues on the Table,* Centre for Foreign Policy Studies, Dalhousie University, Halifax.

Index